The Deepest of Pain

The Deepest of Pain

by
B.Y. Disney
(Beatrice Yvonne Disney)

Edited by
Donna Morscher

E-BookTime, LLC
Montgomery, Alabama

The Deepest of Pain

Library of Congress Control Number: 2006931519

ISBN: 1-59824-318-7

First Edition
Published August 2006
E-BookTime, LLC
6598 Pumpkin Road
Montgomery, AL 36108
www.e-booktime.com

Dedication of this book...

First to GOD
Second to DAD
Third to RAYMOND

Contents

Contents

Stories and Poems for Friends

Contents

Poems for Friends of Friends

Contents

Thank You

Many thanks go out to some special people for their love and support in the completion of this book. Without the help of the following people this book could not have been completed.

JOAN MORTON........for typing all the stories and poems for Yvonne and turning them over to our family after Yvonne's death. Without these transactions this book could not have been published in Yvonne's name.

LEONARD PROFFITT.......my brother-in-law and friend of Yvonne's for all his knowledge and assistance with the computer and transposing of the poems.

MARGIE HARRISON....Yvonne's dear friend who invited me into her home to help me with the finalization of this book. Her input helped me tremendously and I am thankful for all her e-mails, information on publishers and support during this past year.

ALEX MAROTTI........for the beautiful drawing on the front of the book. This was Yvonne's choice to have mother and child expressing "The Deepest of Pain."

THOMAS MORSCHER........my sweet husband and best brother-in-law to my sister. For allowing me to take her on mini-vacations, spending hours on the phone with her and many hours away from him while completing her book.

Foreword

I am writing this book for two reasons. God told me to and help others grieving pain. I have been writing Inspirational Verses for years for those who had lost a loved one, and reading them as part of their eulogy. Many have told me how much they were touched by them and I should put them into a book to reach the thousands who are going through the same hell as we all faced.

The first year after my dad's death, he came to me in a vision dream. In the book, I share the vision and the poem my dad said to me. He told me that it was God's will for me to use the talent God had given me..." to reach into mans soul...then happiness you'll behold." I have been writing poems through the years. I know that there is more I could have done to help those as God wills. Too bad it takes a brick wall to fall on us before we heed God's call.

My "brick wall" was the death of my son, Raymond, six and a half years ago. When Ray died, I never knew that a human could have, and be able to handle, so much pain. (Now, I fully understand..." God doesn't give us more than we can handle.") If one has not gone through the fire, it is impossible to explain the hell parents go through. Yet, I can truly say that Ray's death gave me back my life! I hadn't been living my life as a Christian, (as I had been raised) and sad to say, it took this horrific tragedy to bring me to my knees. I, like most, blamed God for not "saving" my son. In the book, I tell of his story and how I realized that he was "saved" when he died. I knew that Ray had been saved from the pits of hell, and was "home," preparing our mansion for my homecoming. I know without God's strength and love, (as in the poem "footprints") carrying me through my storm,

I couldn't have faced this *The Deepest of Pain*, (which is the title God gave me for "our" book.)

Another thing I began to realize is that many of the parents did not know the Lord. This occurred to me when they were asking me how I got through my son's death. My honest reply was always—only by the grace of God, or, with God's strength—something on that reference. By the look on their face, it was evident they didn't have a clue what I was talking about. It really didn't dawn on me until then how blessed I truly was to know the Lord and to have His strength to get me through each day and night! I had a sinking feeling in the pit of my stomach as I looked into the eyes of these lost, pleading parents. How do they get through this without your help, Lord. I'd prayed. They don't even have the peace to know that they can see their child again if he, or she was saved and if they too accepted Jesus Christ as their Lord and Savior. Only God knows if our child was saved for sure, unless we raised our child to know God but even if not, they can always accept Him into their hearts on their death bed and their heavenly Father will extend his hands, bringing them into His Kingdom for a joyous life eternal. To have the peace to know that I will hold my son again, for all of eternity gives me the strength to face another day and I want others to know this peace also—and, so does God.

The poems within the book are of any child that the Lord has put into my life, directly or indirectly. They include some well-knowns, such as JFK, Jr. and Philip Butcher (son of Sam Butcher the Artist of Precious Moments). I believe God put them upon my heart as their tragedy touched so many lives.

I believe that God creates us all for a purpose and at the time of our birth we are all given a gift, which we are to use to benefit others and to GLORIFY our Lord. I have learned through the years that you cannot out-give the Lord! I am so blessed when one tells me how much my poem touched them or helped them and their family. I make sure that they know that they are the words from God—I am but His instrument—and I tell them to thank God, not me. I am so sorry that it took me so long to heed His call, but I am grateful I finally woke up. When I die and am standing before my Lord and Savior, I want Him to Say, "Well done my good and faithful servant." I have a crochet hanging which reads, "What we are is God's gift to us—what we become is our gift to God."

Beatrice Yvonne Disney

About the Author

Born on November 5th, 1944 in Hamilton, Ohio to the proud parents, Paul "Shorty" and Clara Davis, a beautiful little girl named Beatrice Yvonne Disney. Raised in a Catholic family, the second of seven children. She received the nickname of Sissy since she was my little Sis and I could not say Yvonne. She remained Sissy to me and all our relatives until she reached high school age.

Born eleven months and twelve days apart everyone thought we were twins growing up. This was mainly because grandma made a lot of our clothes and mom dressed us alike. We certainly didn't look alike as Yvonne had straight brown hair and I was a blond full of curls. We were about the same in stature until we reached the 1st grade then Yvonne passed me and I remained the short one.

Our childhood days were full of neighborhood friends, family gatherings, school and church functions and lots of love. We would play with our dolls and sing sons like "Oh Little Playmate," take our dance lessons and practice our new steps all the way home. Skating and sled riding at Potters Park, picnics and dancing at Hoppy's Island, Ford's ball park, playing games with our childhood friends, like kick the can, ditch, and red rover were amongst our favorite things to do. There were six of us who became real buddies and always played together. Now it saddens me to think I am the last of these six friends, including Yvonne, who all died before the age of sixty. It makes me wonder what God has in store for me.

Over the years, Yvonne had written poems for family members for their birthday, anniversary, graduation or any special occasion. She eventually started writing poems for the loss of loved ones.

Our father passed away on November 5, 1975 which was on Yvonne's birthday. She considered it an honor to celebrate her birth and his rebirth on the same day. She became inspired, as she tells in her book, after a vision from our dad as he gave her "Words From Beyond." She was spiritually directed by the hand of the Lord through her hand and God's lips to her ear. She has been an inspiration to many who have lost a child. It was through the loss of her son, as she felt "The Deepest of Pain", that she was to abide by her father through her heavenly Father to help others with her God given talent.

Yvonne's life consisted of helping others in need, even though she had so little and gave so much. This was expressed by our sister Pam in a poem written to Yvonne at the time of her death. Known to many as the Hat Lady, as she always dressed with a hat, she would help all in need.

Yvonne's biggest dream was to complete this book, therefore, I made a promise to myself and my sister's three children that I would complete their mother's book in hope of fulfilling her dream. The end of this book is a poem written and dedicated to Yvonne, by Gary her eldest son, at the time of her death.

Even though we were miles apart, our hearts were together. I miss my beloved sister, especially our phone conversations, updates on our families, the laughter and prayers together. I hold on to all the fond memories I shared with her as a child, a teenager, a mother, a grandmother and my best friend.

She truly had a HEART of GOLD and is now walking those streets of gold, living in a lighthouse, her mansion in the sky, surrounded by her Ray Ray, father and angel friends.

My prayer for the reader, is that Yvonne's poems will inspire or touch you in the way the Lord inspired her.

"Farewell My Dear Sister," "OUR POETIC ANGEL" until we meet again.

Your Loving Sissy,
Donna

Tributes to Yvonne

Have you ever had a passion so deep within you that you strive forward everyday to bring it to manifest itself? I believe we all have in one degree or another. However, I have never seen anyone more determined to bring a passion to life as my dear friend Yvonne Disney. Yvonne's passion was to live in a lighthouse, preferably in Florida, although, she would have gone wherever the Lord led her.

The purpose of occupying the lighthouse was to provide a place for people who were emotionally hurting due from the loss of a loved one, mainly a child. Indeed, this was the main purpose of the lighthouse. However, she would of taken in the hurting for whatever their reason. The name of the lighthouse was going to be 'Ray's of Hope Refuge'. This was not a name randomly chosen. This particular name was selected because her son Raymond died in her arms at the age of thirty-one from kidney failure.

Therefore, Yvonne knew first hand the pain and sorrow that came with the loss of a child. She always felt that there was an urgent need for more hands-on-help for people dealing with this specific grief. This would not be educated therapeutic help; just heart to heart compassion passed on to bring comfort. Moreover, Yvonne would tell you that Jesus Christ is the number one comforter. She would proclaim that He is the one who provided her with peace over the death of her son. If a person did not know Jesus she would not shun them away. On the contrary, she would gently, yet boldly, tell them her survival story and then give God all the glory. As a result, she would hope that they would accept Jesus into their lives and receive their healing as she did.

In conclusion, it is safe to say that Yvonne had a God given talent, not one to keep to herself, but one to share with the world. This beautiful book of poetry you are about to read was birthed from the desire of Yvonne's heart. She would tell you that this book would be the catalyst to bring in the funds needed to run Ray's of Hope Refuge, and that she would travel wherever she needed to so that she could promote it. Consequently, she will not be able to pursue that promotion. Yvonne died on February 25, 2004 at the age of fifty-nine. Nonetheless, there are family members and friends that want to carry on Yvonne's passion. This is the attempt to do so.

As you read this poetry, may God bring you to a place of comfort.

Margie Harrison

The Poet

Through the years I've written words
   to ease many souls in pain
These are not my words friend
   but I'll tell you the poet's name

On yes, it is I
   who have paper and pen in hand
I am but the instrument
   trying to soothe my fellowman

These words of inspiration
   came from up above
Can you not hear His voice
   in these words of love

Oh how He loves His children
   it breaks His heart to see
When we are in pain
   and feel so helplessly

This is why He tells me
   what He wants you to hear
Too often He talks to us
   but we just close our ears

More often, than not, we blame Him
   for our tragic loss
It was He who gave us eternity
   His Son's death, is what it cost

Yes, He knows our pain friend
  for He felt it too
When His Son, suffered and died
  out of love for me and you

Often, one has asked me how did I
  get through the death of Ray
At first I had a hard time
  because I forgot to pray

I like you, also blamed God
  down deep, I knew I was wrong
My God is a loving and good God
  Satan is where the blame belongs

I came back to realism
  and fell to my knees
I need your strength, dear Lord
  please help me God, please!!

I felt His arms around me
  felt peace within
I knew in my heart
  I'd see my son again

That's why God has chosen me
  to write His words for you
For I know that only He
  can help you pull through

He is known by many names —
  God, Jesus, Holy Spirit too
Master, Father, The Light, Physician
  just to mention a few

He is also called the Comforter
and I will guarantee
No matter what your pain is
He can comfort thee

To me He is "THE POET"
the best one that I know
Sending words of healing
to aching lost souls

I am proud to be His vessel
in anyway I can
He puts His Lips to my ears
His hand upon my hand

I listen very earnestly
to what God wants to say
Before I write a word
silently, I pray

Give me the words, Lord
You want me to say
To give comfort and healing
through the night and day

Open their eyes, Lord —
to see you are the light
Without you, I fear
Satan wins the fight

Let them see, you are the way
to see their child again
That you are their Lord and savior
You are their best friend

I thank you, my Lord
  just for choosing me
To be your instrument
  to offer your Kingdom Keys ...

Food for Thought

When I am ill, I feel depressed... alone... unneeded... unwanted... a Nothing...I wish the day was over... yet dread the tomorrows to come.

I close my eyes and mind to the world and think of my life...my blessings...I ask God to forgive me for feeling sorry for myself...for I know I am not alone... EVER! Tomorrow will be beautiful ...as it was today... for God has made it... and Nothing He has made is ugly...especially me...for I know, He would never take time to make a Nothing!!!

THANK YOU GOD!!!

Dedication to God

First — God —

For blessing me with the gift of writing Inspirational Verse and for allowing me to go through the "Fires" strengthening my character and more importantly my FAITH in my Lord and Saviour, Jesus Christ. I know now, the crises I faced throughout my life were stepping stones leading me to the destination God had created me for. To help those who too have gone through their fires and some eventually as I, through the Deepest of Pain, the lost of their child or even worse, their children.

God

First, to God be the GLORY! Without the gift of writing (Inspirational Verse) which God blessed me with when He created me, this book nor any of these poems within would exist. I truly believe we are given a gift and a purpose for our existence when our Lord creates us. Mine is to use the words which God gives me through Inspirational Verse to try to ease the pain others endure throughout their lives. Especially as they face "The Deepest of Pain," the loss of their child or even more horrifying children through death. Just as important, if not more importantly, to reach into man's soul, to bring them to the realization of God's love for them so that they can one day unite with their loved ones for everlasting—eternal joy in heaven with our Creator, Lord and Savior, Jesus Christ.

Marrying at the early age of sixteen and divorcing by the time I was twenty, with three little ones to support, definitely looked like a hard road ahead of me. My biggest mistake was taking my eyes off of the Lord and trying to handle life alone. With no experience at any type of work, other than a car-hop at the local A&W Rootbeer stand. I lied about my age and made my second mistake. I began cocktail waitressing in a "Go-Go" club. Being young and still naive (even with three kids) I sure grew up fast.

My friend's mother hired me and I knew she knew my real age but she and her daughter, Kathy, were really a big help and very protective of me when the customers tried to get out of hand. I hated the job but my kids and I liked to eat, so I had to grow up quickly, swallow my pride and prayed, "God get me out of this place quick which, He did!"

I soon started working for Isgro's Italian Restaurant, where eventually I felt like part of their family and have remained so all these years. I am so grateful for this blessing from God. I truly believe we choose our own happiness — we make our own choices.

Years ago, I wrote "Life Is Like A Bed Of Roses—all one must do is pick between the thorns to enjoy the true beauty..."Like everything else I have ever written, these words were from God. Strangely enough, until right before I started putting this book together did I fully understand what it meant.

I thought it meant if you were careful—don't get stuck by the thorns—you would enjoy your life—NOT! God revealed to me the true meaning of this statement which I wrote about 30 years ago in the book, He Choose The Nails, by Max Lucado. In the 3rd chapter he explains throughout scripture, thorns symbolize sin, not the consequence of sin. Wow! I can't believe after all these years, that it didn't mean what I thought it meant.

I was watching a concert on TV with Bill and Gloria Gaither and they were talking about a song they wrote called, "Because He Lives".

It was not until they were singing it that God revealed to them what the words truly meant. She said, "Sometimes we write things which we don't even know why until much later when God tells us why we did".

God had just confirmed what He had shown me about the thorns...in God's Time Clock...not ours...His! God's Time Clock is not the same as ours, but trust me, He is ALWAYS on time!

Moving to Florida, for numerous reasons. I thought I'd start a new and better life for myself and my three kids. It didn't take me long to make another mistake, but I thank God for this one every day of my life. Of course, at the time, I didn't look at it as a blessing, but from the time my son Joedy was born, I knew God had answered my prayers.

Being lonely, I asked God to send me a love, I meant a man, but God in His wisdom sent me a lasting Love, that of a child. Of course, I yelled, "WHAT are you doing God?" as though my getting pregnant was ALL His fault—who did I think I was—the Virgin Mary? It wasn't the Immaculate Conception! But like most, I was blaming God for MY mistake.

Now I praise God for letting me choose to keep my beautiful child. God knew this was the best mistake I would ever make. At the time, of course, I couldn't understand why God would punish me with another child. I could hardly feed and take care of the three still VERY little ones I had! There I went again—blaming God for my "mistake." God did NOT tell me to commit sin and go to bed with this man, just as He never makes us do anything we don't choose to do with FREE WILL. So why do we always blame Him? As mere humans, we have to blame someone, other than ourselves, so why not God? If He is so powerful, why didn't He prevent me from getting pregnant? AGAIN—God is NOT a dictator! We are NOT puppets on a string controlled by our CREATOR!

I have found through the years that I learned more through my mistakes than my triumphs, which is why I'm revealing my soul, to show that when we make mistakes or when something bad happens to us, we want to BLAME God!

Back to my mistakes. The restaurant/bar business was good to me, as in good I mean lucrative enough to support us five, but it destroyed me in about every other aspect of my life. At most jobs, I'd work late but was too hyper to go home and go straight to sleep, so I'd go to a bar to relax—"to come down"—so I could get my much needed rest. This was how I rationalized drinking a fifth or more of whatever booze I could get my hands on almost every night. Like anything we do in life, we don't start out with the intention to become a drunk, or to neglect our kids, self family and especially God. But one thing led to the next and after years of this routine, I found myself in a pickle—or should I say I got pickled almost every night Of course, at the time I thought I was handling it all just great.

Soon the drinking led to all night partying, with one man or a house full of drunks, like me. I would do great to get home before the kids woke up and later in time to get them off to school so I could sleep the whole day in order to get ready to start my same ruthless routine over and over again. No wonder I was so miserable, as I look back at it now with sober eyes.

I, like most, thought my knight in shinning armor would ride into that bar and rescue me from all this madness. Now, I realize if he had he probable would have been so drunk, he would have fallen off the horse before he rescued me. What was I thinking? I was truly a tortured person and didn't even know how tortured at the time.

I loved my kids very much and I did do things for and with them but I didn't see how much I was hurting them by showing them the way you shouldn't live. I regret this more than anything, especially since they, like their mom, enjoyed the bar scene as much as I when they were of age—and even before becoming of age.

This especially haunts me about Raymond, my second child who had his first kidney operation at the age of eleven. I can still hear his doctor say, "Ray, as long as you don't drink when you get older, you will probably live a normal life." Those words still haunt me as I think how many times Ray poured himself into the bottle, just like his mom did. As Ray's mother, I didn't believe—or should I say—refused to believe that Raymond would die at an early age. I was his mother—I would die before him.

Of course as all kids think, Ray thought he was invincible. It took a few more operations, years of denial, partying and gallons of more booze before we realized Dr. Witta's fear would come true. After Ray's last operation in December of '93,his surgeon told us that he gave Ray only six months to live. That was truly the first time I think I really believed it would happen—and so did Raymond, but we both knew it was way too late to start accepting his fate.

Some things had changed through the years before we reached this final stretch in the road. I finally let God back into my life and reached out to Him instead of the bottle and found out that although I had left God, He had never left me. How sad it is that the only time we go to God is when we need His help—especially in a tragedy such as I was facing. Being the loving, forgiving Father that He is, I knew He was there just waiting for me to ask for his strength. Just as in the poem, "Footprints," He not only was by my side all my life but in times such as now, He "CARRIED" me through the "FIRES."

We make our own choices, whether they be good or bad and those choices bring us to where we are in life. We can't live in the "middle" of life. The middle of Life is IF. If only I had done that—or, if I would've, If I could've—IF—IF—IF. There is no such animal, after the fact—too late to go back and change what we have already done, but trust me, it's not too late to change our future. God has already forgiven us of all our sins, but we must know Jesus as our Lord and Savior to have the real JOY that He wants us to have in this life. More importantly for eternal life with Him and our loved ones in God's kingdom.

It was a long hard road trying to raise four children but that was because I chose that road—not God or anyone else. I know now if I had kept my eyes on the Lord— let go and let God—my travel would have been a lot easier to handle. I didn't say a lot easier—I said to handle. Just because you are a Christian doesn't mean you don't have struggles, but with God there to help, makes it bearable.

As I said previously, I didn't see it then but now I see my mistakes as stepping stones, carefully laid to bring me to the destination God created me for. I thank God that I finally realize this and I will turn my bad into good by using the gift of writing He blessed me with to try to open the eyes and hearts of those who like me, are going through their "fires" in life—especially, "The Deepest of Pain."

God has put so many people in my life since my son's death who also have lost a child or children and now I know why I went through that most trying trial. Unless you've experienced it first hand, you can't possibly grasp the immeasurable pain a parent endures at that time. God knows that pain too as He watched His Son, Jesus, suffer and die on the cross out of the love He has for all of us, His children. How deep is that love? Could you give your child up to die for someone else? I don't think I ever could.

After losing their child, many asked me how did I handle it. "With the grace of God," I replied. Many looked at me as though I had three heads which made me realize they had no idea what I was saying.

In most cases, they didn't know God and those who did were hurting so much that they blamed God for not saving their child—just as I had. Yes, even as a Christian, one who had been taught the love of God all my life, was now turning my back on God and blaming Him just as I had for all my misfortunes throughout my entire life. How could I expect people who never were taught of God's love, to understand what I was saying. Trust in God—pray for his strength—He only gives us what we can handle—when a door shuts, a window opens—WHAT was I saying to these poor hurting souls!

I know I felt like I was the only one who ever had or would experience this type of DEEP pain. I felt like no one could possibly understand. I felt like I just couldn't breathe—I couldn't get my breath! There was just NO way I would EVER, EVER, get through this Pain—this LOSS! But there was and is for each of us who also feel the same as I That way is the only WAY. His name is Jesus.

Finally coming to my senses, I fell to my knees and ASKED God to HELP me! That's all—I just ASKED! What an awesome God...He answered. That is why with God's hand upon mine, His lips to my ears, we are writing this book to try to help the lost souls to see that there is hope in our tomorrows, to show that we are not alone in our sorrow, or in our pleas for help. He knows how many are hurting and feel so alone and helpless because they faced "The Deepest of Pain" as I have.

I soon realized that although the death of a child was the factor, the way they died was different in almost every case. Who is to say which is the worst way to lose your child whether it be a shocking quick accident or a long awaiting, such as I watching my son die a slow painful death.

When I read the Adam Walsh story, my heart broke for that family as I thought about the hell they must have gone through waiting for the news of the death of their child. It became even more real when Pam, a woman from my church, was comforting me and told me about her son, who had run away and for a whole year waited for the outcome, which sad to say also was death. No matter how we lose our kids, the pain couldn't cut any deeper.

The poems within are the actual poems I wrote. When each of these parents faced their hardest trial on this earth. These were the words God gave me to give them and I believe He wants me to share them with each of you in hopes to show you that you are not alone and there is a way to help ease your pain.

You will never get over the pain, nor will you ever forget that child, but you can be grateful that God shared him or her with you for the time that He did and someday you will be united with them again, forever.

Introduction

After birthing four children, I once stated that labor pains had to be the worst pain anyone could possibly endure, especially after I had Raymond, my second child. I was anemic and couldn't be given a sedative for fear I wasn't strong enough to come out of it. The pain was excruciating! That was way before Lamaze was heard of. Even my afterbirth pains felt like labor pains!

My poor baby was so sick from the time he came into this world, being born anemic, caused by me and eleven years later, finding out he was born with only one kidney which was also damaged.

Thirty-one years later my statement about pain was to smack me in the face as I realized it was far from the truth. Birthing a child was far easier than burying one! On June 9, 1994, I held my son Raymond as he took his final breath. He blew his last two breaths into my face and his whole life, from the time of his painful birth through his entire sick life, flashed through my mind as I watched my son die. That is the worst pain anyone can face — "The DEEPEST of Pain!"

Ray's death was a life changing experience for me. Being raised in a good Christian family, my parents taught me the fear and love of God. I was taught the teachings of the Bible in the Catholic school and church but I can honestly say, I didn't have a "relationship" with Jesus Christ, nor, did I know anything about having the power of the Holy Spirit.

After my divorce, church became less of a priority. I still prayed, especially when I needed help from the Lord, but I am sorry to say, I was too busy with work, kids and partying to take the time to worship the One I needed most in my life.

When Raymond was eleven I got my wake-up call. He had to have an emergency kidney operation and it was then they discovered how severe his illness was. The fear of losing him brought me to my knees, pleading with the Lord whom I'd forgotten, but my loving, merciful Father had never forsaken me. He carried me through my really rough times.

Raymond's illness also brought me back to my love of writing Inspirational Verses. I had written some poetry for friends for their birthdays, anniversary, or other such occasions. My Inspirational Verses, as well as the Lord had been put on the back burner. I had tried to ease my pain through alcohol and partying, out of fear of losing my most precious gem, but until I let my Lord wrap His loving arms around me, could I face the possibility of Raymond's death. I began seeing, the more Inspirational Verses I wrote for others, the more peace of mind, God gave to me. This became even more evident after Raymond's death. God put more and more families into my life that were hurting as I was from the death of their child, or even worse children.

"Words from Beyond," was a poem I had written after my dad came to me in a "Vision" dream (explained further in the book). These words began to disturb me as I knew for years God had been wanting me to use the gift He had given me. My reason for being on this earth is to help others go THROUGH the fire—not stay in it, as so many do. Too bad, I thought it takes a tragedy like the death of my son to yield to the will of the Lord.

Now, I not only regularly attend church, I joined and learned what it meant to have a relationship with Jesus Christ. I found a forgiving, loving and caring Heavenly Father. I felt his warmth and strength with me daily. As I progressed in my faith and walk, I felt the power of the Holy Spirit enhancing my strength to face the tomorrows and enlighten the love of my Lord and Savior, Jesus Christ. Only then, did I come to realize how Spiritually directed my poems were. They were truly the hand of the Lord—not mine!

My poems were being read as eulogies for people I had never met but was asked by family members to write words of comfort for their hurting loved ones. I was paid immensely—not with money—but more importantly with gratitude by letting me know how my poem helped them to let go and let God ease their pain. I take no credit for these words, I give All the GLORY to God, as I am only His instrument. I have no doubt they are the words of the Lord, as I often have to read what I just wrote to know what I wrote. They often bring me to tears and I am awed of His love and grace shown through my writings. I am honored that God allows me to be His instrument in helping in the healing of His lost sheep.

In most cases, I was talking to non-believers but even those who knew the Lord were questioning where was He when my child was dying? As a Christian, I questioned God many times as why my son was so sick and dying. I was pleading out of desperation as any mother would to save her son, just as Mary did when she watched in horror as her Son, Jesus, was beaten and crucified for us. I, nor anyone has the answer as to why. If it isn't revealed on this earth, it will be in the Kingdom when we go "home" to our Lord and we join our loved ones again. Halleluiah!

I do know that our God is a loving Father and as most of our earthly fathers, does not want us to hurt for any reason. What an awesome God we serve

God did not make us puppets on a string to do only as He willed but I do know now there are numerous reasons why we make the wrong choices in life which often causes us our own demise—but trust me, God is NOT the problem—He is the Answer. We all know that there is good and bad in this world—we must choose— God is GOOD —

Satan is BAD—Satan is the prince of this world. It is evident in everything we see and hear in this world today. It is up to us—we have a free will— it is our choice—What will be yours tomorrow?

When God got kicked out of schools in 1963, Satan came slithering in! Teenage pregnancies went on a rise as well as abortions and rapes. Drugs became a way of life and kids killing kids was too often seen on the streets as well as in the schools. Someone once said, "Grass was something in my time that we mowed, pot was a pan for cooking, coke was a cold drink and aids was something you did to help someone!" These words all take on a new meaning in the American language with our kids today. Morals is a word they have to look up in the dictionary for the meaning and the name of God is only called upon in vain.

Chewing gum use to be the #1 problem in school and kids disturbing kids was #2. Disagreements were handled with fists not knives and guns! R-E-S-P-E-C-T wasn't just a song, it was what was expected from kids for their elders, peers and for themselves!

I believe pornography has become our worst nightmare in trying to raise decent, God-fearing kids in today's world. It is found on our TV, theaters, the internet, adult movie houses, and trash magazines sold in almost any store on every corner.

If that isn't enough to corrupt our kids, the adults will show them how to kill their babies through abortions and/or abuse, and when they feel their elders should no longer live for one reason or another, they will kill them too trying to legally call it euthanasia.

Giving Thanks

When I was a little girl
  we didn't have very much
I mean in material things
  like in riches and such

Why we didn't even have a car
  but that didn't stop us
Sometimes we would walk
  or ride the city bus

Our clothes — they were nice
  some our grandma made
And we always looked special
  on all the Holidays

We didn't go to too many places
  other than to baseball games
Or maybe window-shopping
  or a movie of some fame

When I got a little older
  about eleven or twelve
We didn't have much then —
  but I thought, my life was swell

We had lots of friends
  to play games in the hood
I wish kids today —
  just understood

I was so happy then —
   no drugs around
No fear of playing
   and getting shot down

When I was a teenager
   life really was great
We moved to a new house
   WOW! What a place!

It looked like a castle
   compared to before
The yard was huge
   and a toilet on the first floor

At first it was just a house
   then it became our home
As warm laughter filled
   from the floor to the dome

We still had very little
   when it came to earthly goods
But we had what we needed
   Dad did the best he could

Sometimes we got a Special treat
   if in came "42"
He'd bring home Frisch's Big Boy
   that's what sweet Dad would do

And after working two jobs
   making it a long day
Dad stopped to buy us "treats"
   somewhere along the way

They'd be on the table
  when we got up for school
But no eating 'til lunch
  was Dad's golden rule

Daddy had a motto
  at which we all did live
A Family stays together who prays together
  it taught us to love and give

I think Dad was right
  as I take a look here
The love within this family
  is strong and sincere

Always there for each other
  the way Daddy was for all
And if one is in trouble
  on the family they can call

Another lesson Daddy taught us
  the most important I believe
Is we can always call on God
  He will always help thee

It may not be the answer
  we were hoping to hear
But Father knows best —
  I promise my dears

Now that I have grown
  I look back and see
How blessed I have been
  to have this family

I think about my childhood
   when I was a little girl
I think I was rich
   although SIS got the curls

We had so much love
   from our Mom and Dad
Today, most kids world
   is really pretty sad

And those little surprises
   no — they weren't much
But to us they said "LOVE"
   from Daddy's loving touch

My Love and Gratitude to the Best Family

As I previously stated, God was my Rock through Raymond's illness and especially his death. I was also blessed with a loving and caring family, who was here for me, especially my sister, Donna.

When Ray was in his final months, he said he would love to see his grandma (my mom) before he died. It had been a long time since Ray had seen mom since she hated to fly and had only been to Florida one time in the twenty-two years that we had lived here. We had only been back to Ohio about three times. I told Donna about Ray's wish and about a week later she called with the surprising news. Our younger sister, Pam and she were going to bring mom to see her grandson. Mom had agreed to fly after she heard it was Ray's wish and she knew he wasn't able to fly to see her. I was ecstatic and Ray had tears in his eyes when I told him the unexpected news. It broke their hearts when they saw how bad Ray looked.

Ray's poor body was so bruised and sore from dialysis that you had to be very careful when you hugged him. Nonetheless, I was as glad as they were to have given Ray his wish. I was especially thankful to Donna for making it possible.

I look at the pictures of their last visit with Ray and it fills my heart with joy and pain as I see how sick my child was, yet it reminds me how great God is that He took my son home to free him of that pain. I am blessed to have a family who cares so much! Thank you, God!

Since Ray's death, sis Donna is still there for me in so many ways. There hasn't been a holiday, my birthday, Ray's death date, or any occasion that she hasn't sent me a gift in his memory, signed, love, Ray. Ray wasn't much of an artist, but he loved to draw me a single red rose, so Donna usually gives me a rose of some type, whether it be a pin, earrings, other jewelry, or an artificial rose in some form. Through the years, she has been very creative and given some beautiful, unique, rose gifts. These gifts given to me in Ray's name has brought me great joy.

On the first anniversary of Ray's death, Sis came to Florida to be with me to help ease the pain and she has called on every anniversary since.

Another blessing was the year Donna took me to the Precious Moment Chapel in Missouri along with 31 other members of the Precious Moment Club. We had the pleasure of meeting Sam Butcher, the artist of the Precious Moment figurines. He signed the numerous mementos the 31 Club Members purchased and we all had our pictures taken with him at a special luncheon, where I presented him with a poem I had written for his precious son Phillip who had passed away. What a memorable trip, thanks to my thoughtful sister, Donna.

It is so important for family to be there for you when you are going through the worst pain in your life. I pray if you have lost a child, your family is there for you, or if you know of someone going through this horrific pain, be there for them, especially at the time of their anniversaries.

All my six brothers, sisters, their spouses, my mom, and numerous relatives were so strong for me throughout this terrible ordeal. I thank them and I thank God for blessing me with the best family I could ever have.

Dedication to Dad

Second — Dad —

All of us have a loving and caring Father in heaven but not everyone was as blessed with a father on earth who gave unconditional love as my daddy did. His love and Faith in God was shown in his daily life and was instilled in all of his children. My dad was my hero and for that I am so grateful. Even when I strayed from God, just as in the story of the "Prodigal Son," he never left me and was waiting there with open arms. Without these early teachings, I don't know if I could have handled my "fires" the way that I did, without getting burnt. I do know, I'm glad I won't have to find out as my love for God is stronger since the lost of my son ... Thanks to the love of both my Fathers.

Dad

One of the fondest childhood memories is the early morning scurrying down the stairs to see what "goodies" dad had left on the kitchen table for us kids. The little bags of chips, candy bars or other snacks were only about 5 cents, but to us they were a gift of love. Dad stopped every night to buy these treats to show his kids that he was thinking of us.

His day began at 5:00am, church at 6:00am, work at 7:00am til 4:00pm, then home to eat, shower and rest for one hour or play baseball in the backyard with his sons then off to his second job in Kentucky (the horse tracks) til about midnight, stop for snacks, if lucky, home in bed by 1:00am so he could get a few hours rest before his day started again! Whew! I'm worn out just writing this! God Bless him!

It saddens me when I see the abuse kids get from their dads today or just the neglect, or lack of love. Even as a kid, I knew how blessed I was to have such a caring father. Child abuse wasn't heard about so much in the '50's, but I still could see how extra special my dad was compared to other kid's dads. Dad wasn't the type to hug and kiss his kids all the time or even to say, "I love you," but his actions spoke loud and clear.

Dad's love for God was also shown in his daily words and actions. He truly put God first, family second, and his fellowman third. The family that prays together, stays together was dad's motto (which proved true in the years to come). No matter how busy dad or any of us were, we took the time to go to our knees as a family unit and give thanks for our blessings. The love of our Heavenly Father was deeply instilled by our earthly father which stayed with me even when I strayed in my coming years. I knew in my heart no matter what I had done, my earthly dad loved and forgave me, so did my Heavenly Father. He would always be there to help if only I'd ask.

Dad's love for others was seen in the work he did for the church charity organizations, a needy neighbor, co-worker or whoever God put in sight of my dad, no matter race or creed, he helped, even if it meant doing without himself. (Remember this was in the 50's when prejudice was very active. Even after my dad had his car hit with rocks driving through a black area late at night after work, he still never showed hatred towards them or anyone of a different race).

I deeply admired my dad throughout my whole life. I don't ever remember him saying a bad word against anyone or ever hearing a bad word said against him. He showed respect towards everyone and they showed him respect in return.

Dad died at the young age of 54 (two weeks short of his 55th birthday). Because he was well known, involved in sports, participated in church functions, employed at Mosler Safe Company and Kentucky Race Tracks for years, he had one of the largest funerals ever held in our small town of Hamilton, Ohio.

My love for dad was so strong that I was in fear of his death. I couldn't bear to think of him out of my life. When you are just a kid, fifty looks old. I think I feared his death for many years, not just when he got older. I believe that was why I decided to move to Florida, stupidly thinking it would be easier if I wasn't around my family all the time. I wouldn't miss them as much when they died.

In late October of 1975, I started having "Vision" dreams about dad, every night for two weeks. I saw dad falling from a ladder, awakening before he hit the ground. Even though he didn't die in my dreams, I knew this was going to happen to him and that he would die. A few days before my birthday, my aunt and uncle came to the house to tell me my worst nightmare had come true. Dad had fallen off a ladder, cleaning the house gutters and was in a coma, breathing by artificial machines. At the precise moment of their news, a large black and white clock appeared on a blank wall with both hands on twelve. I knew my dad would die at either midnight or noon.

Leaving immediately for Ohio, I prayed on the plane, asking God to help my family through this worst ordeal we would probably ever have to face. As much as I wanted my dad to live, I knew in my heart, he wouldn't I knew the reason for the dreams was God's way of preparing me, (the best one can prepare) for the death of someone I loved so very much.

Upon my arrival at the hospital, my heart broke as I watched my mom in complete denial at the possibility of her loving husband's passing. "He is too young! He is such a good person, he has seven kids and his youngest child is just thirteen," mom would say. It made me think back to daddy's prayers, asking God to let him live at least long enough for all of his kids to reach their teenage years, so they would be old enough to help themselves and not depend on mom so much. It was as though he had a feeling he would die young and didn't want mom to be burdened with a houseful of small children. She had never worked outside of the home, thus, all she knew was housework and kids.

After a family prayer in the hospital chapel, God led me to write my farewell poem to daddy. I went into the I.C.U. and read it to him. Although still in a coma, I know he could hear the words God told me to write. "I know you'll be with God before the next rising sun...." it read. A priest came in as I read it and said, "I hear tomorrow is your birthday. How are you going to feel if he dies on your day?" "As bad as if it were today or the day after," I said quickly. "I will miss him deeply." Then I said, "Actually, I would be honored if God takes daddy home on my birthday, so that we can share his rebirth and my birth on the same day." Silently, I thought, how ironic that God would choose November 5th, my "B" day. No one but God knew how I felt about sharing this day with my dad. You see, I always felt left out of the birthday celebrations in November.

My dad's, sister Donna, and brother Bobby's birthdays were on November 22nd, 23rd, and 24th, which were always celebrated on Thanksgiving Day. Every year I felt left out, since mine was on November 5th. I had my own little celebration. I know it sounds stupid—most would want their very own day—that's what birthdays are— your special day, right? Well, I was always a little strange—I felt jealous—like not a part of the family—left out—well, you get the idea—I hope. Anyway, God got it and I believe even if it was stupid on my part, God fixed it in the end—the best way anyone could. What an awesome God! Now on November 5th as I arise, I say, "Happy Birthday, Daddy!"

By the way, dad's death certificate read T.O.D. 12:01 (noon) as God had revealed to me in Florida. Why dad died so early, we won't know until God reveals that in this life or our next. In my heart, I don't believe God caused his death, but He did give us all the strength to endure the pain and to continue our lives with the love for God that daddy would've wanted us to.

God's gift of love kept on giving even after my daddy's death. Having strayed from church but never losing complete sight of God's love through my life of living in a world of Satan, God once again sent my dad to give me a wake-up call. I don't remember exactly when, but about two years after dad died, he came to me in a "Vision" dream. He stood at the foot of my four poster antique bed, dressed in a trench coat and hat, I so loved him in when I was a small child. He looked at me very seriously and said the words I later wrote down and titled, "Words From Beyond," shown on the forthcoming page. After reciting these words, he smiled the smile I so dearly loved and missed and slowly floated backwards, disappearing into thin air.

I woke up, sitting straight up, shaking inwardly—not outwardly—with cold sweat pouring off me. Following my normal procedure with my "vision" dreams, I looked at the clock, and as usual it was 2:00am. I grabbed the pen and paper I always keep on my bed stand (for such times as this) and wrote the words my dad had just spoken to me. I remember (as though it happened yesterday), I lay down after writing it and fell quickly back to sleep as though nothing had happened.

The next morning, I awoke and immediately thought, dad was here last night! Again, I sat straight up in bed and quietly repeated over and over, as if in disbelief myself, but I knew wholeheartedly, I did have a visit from my dad! I looked at my nightstand and there was the notepad with his words I retrieved. It was as though I was afraid it would disappear if I didn't read fast. The hair on my body from head to toe stood straight up! It all came back to me! Dad in his coat and hat, his words, his smile—Wow! How great is my God, I thought that He would allow dad to come to me even after his death. It was especially great, I thought, since I wasn't even living a Christian life, which is exactly why He sent him I thought—to wake me up—to the misguided ways I was living. Use God's gift—reach into man's soul— happiness you'll behold—The words would haunt me for a while, but so sad to say it would be years before I was to truly take heed of my Lord's warning given to me through my dad.

For a while I got back into writing Inspirational Verses for a needy friend or even a needy stranger, but until the death of my son, I don't think I realized what God had been so desperately trying to get me to comprehend for my sake, as well as to benefit those who needed God's strength through their "Deepest of Pain." So sad, it took the death of my son to open my eyes and my heart to the ONES who love me more and want nothing but the best for me—my Heavenly Father and my earthly dad.

A Farewell Note of Love

A farewell poem, Daddy, just for you,
   from all your loved ones
Of your whole life through

We'll miss you dearly,
   Words can't explain
Strength we will find,
   Our faith retain

Peace of Heart, Body and Soul.
   'Tis what you want
for us we all know

We've accepted God's Will,
   What must be done
We know you'll be with Him,
   before the next sun

We love you, sweet Dad,
   this you know
Your thoughts will be with us,
   your strength and glow

Our farewells we will say,
   but only for now
Your memories and love,
   We'll always endow

We know you'll be happy,
  and that's what counts
We'll carry on strongly,
  so have no doubts

God will take care of us,
  the family and me
And life will be easier,
  when "VISIONS" we see

Your Loving Daughter
Yvonne

In Memory of Dad Words from Beyond

I closed my eyes and wandered
  Into the neverland of sleep
My body was restless
  When words I heard speak

Daughter! Daughter!
  What is they worth
When nothing you will do
  With the talent God's given you
    To share with others too

  Poetry is in your heart
    To reach into man's soul
  Let the words from you depart
    Then happiness you'll behold

Dedication to Raymond

Third — Raymond —

My beloved son, Ray-Ray. His life and death opened my eyes and heart to the depth of God's love and the depth of pain endured when a child precedes their parent(s) in death. I could not let my son's death be in vain, thus, using my God-given gift. I pray the poems within touch the heart and soul of those, who like I, have faced "The Deepest of Pain." He was truly my Ray-Ray of sunshine.

In Loving Memory of Raymond

It had been five months since my son had his last kidney removed, which has been causing infections throughout his body. Five months watching him exist—not live—in misery and pain. Five months since his doctor gave him a six month sentence to live. Every time he asked, "Why doesn't God just let me die, mom?" my heart would break. "I guess He doesn't think you are ready, honey,"—not really knowing how to answer the same question I had been asking God. He was so miserable. Completely bed-ridden except for his trips to the doctors and three times a week for his dialysis treatments, Ray's bedroom was his entire world. Thank God he loved to watch TV, especially the old westerns and the nostalgic stations to keep his mind occupied. Nonetheless, I knew the thought of dying was never far from his thought.

Raymond's illness became so severe that my daughter, who is a nurse, insisted that we put Ray in a nursing home. Which Ray and I were against.

I couldn't stand to see him in there with those eighty and up senior citizens with him being just thirty-one and him crying and pleading every night for me to please bring him home with me.

I knew Ray was in his final stage of life and I wasn't going to allow him to die in a strange place. There was nothing else to do but kidnap him out of that place. So I quit my job and gave Ray around the clock care to make him as comfortable as possible in his last days.

Lisa was not too happy with me but Ray and I were very happy. There wasn't a lot I could do to make his life easier, except I could cook his favorite food. Some days he'd be too sick to eat but when he could, whatever he wanted (and was allowed on his diet), I would make it for him. Ray loved his mama's cooking and it gave me great pleasure to do this little thing for him. Every night he'd say the same thing—"Mom, this is the best dinner you ever cooked." Then we would all laugh as we still do when the kids say this out of love and in memory of Ray.

It was hard to watch my child so helpless. A child who loved life—loved to live! His love for life was part the reason for his early demise. He loved to be with people, partying and dancing in the bars until the wee hours of the morning. Like his mother, he too was in the bar/restaurant business and enjoyed the night life. Needless to say the guilt of my contribution to my child's death still haunts me. Maybe he'd still be alive if I had been a better role model of IF I had been going to church instead of the bars—IF I had taught him more about the love of God instead of the love of partying—IF—IF—IF—gain, the middle of LIFE—is IF. We can't live in the middle of what already has been—but it doesn't stop the guilt trip. I know that Ray, like all of us, had free will and knowing his type of character, he probably would have chosen the same life style without any influences from me. But like all parents, we go through a deep guilt trip, blaming ourselves in one way or another for our child's death. We live in the middle of LIFE—If—only I did this— IF—I didn't do that—IF—I should've—IF—I would've—IF—IF—IF—!!

The following month was June—the SIXTH month! Maybe the doctor is wrong, I'd say to myself. They aren't always right—100%—just because he said six— doesn't mean exactly six—I was still in denial of my son dying. I knew Raymond had been taught the love of God throughout his life but he hadn't lived his life as a Christian for the most of it. I still feared where he would spend eternity. The thought of him not going to heaven to be with the Lord kept me from letting go, to set him free to die.

The first week of June, my brother, Paul, and his wife Pam came from Ohio to see us. "Sis, God told me to come here to take Ray to be completely healed at the Benny Hinn Ministry," he said. A COMPLETE healing, I thought. The only time you get a complete healing is when you die and go to heaven and the Lord gives you a new body—no more pain—no illness—no suffering—a whole new body. "No," I said, "I don't want him to go. It's his dialysis day, he can't go." "I want to go," Raymond cried. "Please mom, I want to go—I can miss my treatment—I know God wants me to go there." I reluctantly gave in and helped load up the car for our travel to Orlando to the Benny Hinn Ministry.

With Paul at the wheel, Ray lounged out on the passenger side and Pam and I in the back, we said a prayer for protection and headed for the interstate. About fifteen minutes into the drive, Ray, in his raspy, low voice said something which none of us understood "What did you say, Raymond?" we all asked. Again, Ray struggled to repeat what he desperately needed to tell us. Still not comprehending, Ray tried to say it slower and louder. Poor Ray, he could hardly talk and none of us understood what he was saying.

Suddenly, Paul said, "Oh no! Sis, didn't you bring something for him to pee in? He said he doesn't have a pot to PISS in." A pot to pee in Paul? Ray doesn't have any kidneys—he's wearing a bag—he doesn't need a pot. By then Ray was really getting frustrated with all of us as I'm sure we sounded like the three stooges— "Who's on First" program. "NO, NO, I mean I have NOTHING—I haven't a Pot to PISS in!" he said as loud as he could. Suddenly, we all became very quiet. Realizing what he was saying, we all busted out laughing. My poor baby. He was quietly lying in the car thinking about dying and realized he had nothing to show for his life. He was using an old saying—I have nothing—not even a pot to piss in!

My heart broke for him as I just gave him a little hug and kiss to say it was all right. Paul said, "Well buddy, you won't need anything in heaven. God has everything there you will need and since we can't take anything with us when we die, why worry about what we have here on earth. Right Ray?" "I've never seen a U-Haul on the back of a hearse." I said, "Besides if one dies and goes to hell, they wouldn't need money as it would burn, and in heaven you won't need it as God supplies all our needs," I said, trying to cheer him up. I guess our answers appeased him as he slept the whole way.

After eating and resting in a nearby hotel, we left early to find the church where we had so often watched as Benny Hinn healed hundreds of broken bodies, minds and souls through the hands of Jesus Christ. My mind rushed with fear and excitement at the same time as we reached the building. Arriving early, my brother went to find a wheelchair and ask for assistance. Their staff was very accommodating and helped us into the back room to pray over him before the service began, which we accepted. About seven of the staff, including Benny Hinn's brother, William, circled around Ray with hands on him as they all began to pray. A Holy spiritual feeling filled the room as the prayers flowed for at least fifteen to twenty minutes.

I couldn't begin to repeat what all they were saying but I know I felt a peace about Ray's dying that I had never felt. Ray looked at me with a look of relief which also I had never seen in him and said, "Mom, I just received the Holy Spirit. I am ready to go 'HOME' to see Jesus." He continued praying with them with his hands extended to the Lord.

The service was about to start out front so we found seats in the back of the room anticipating an early exit Raymond had a tailbone injury from years before and his time limit for sitting was only about twenty minutes, which he had already exceeded. I got Raymond settled and left him with Paul and Pam so I could go outside to gather my thoughts. I was pretty blown away with his statement about going "HOME" to see Jesus and felt a need to be alone with the Lord. With a star-filled sky to light the night, I cried out to God through tearful eyes. "I now know Lord why you haven't taken my son home, Ray has been ready—it is I who wasn't. I was so fearful he wouldn't be in heaven with you, Lord, I just couldn't let go. Now, I see the reason for this trip here. It wasn't for Raymond, it is for me. I just couldn't let him go until I knew that he would be in the arms of his heavenly Father." My heart was at peace as I had seen and heard my son say he was ready and for the first time, I knew he was. "He is all yours," I said through teary eyes," bring him home to you, Lord. Give him freedom for all his pain." How awesome is our God, I thought. He wouldn't take Ray home until I had peace with it—until I was ready to surrender him back to his Maker.

About two hours later, Raymond had proved me wrong. He had been sitting with no tailbone pain or anything else hurting him. That in itself was a miracle! One the way back to the hotel, we stopped by Taco Bell, one of Raymond's favorite eateries but he couldn't eat, saying he didn't feel well. We hurried him back to the room and got him ready for bed. It proved to be a long night, as every time we laid him down, he would choke and say he couldn't breathe. After several hours of this and no one able to sleep, I told Paul, "I think he just wants to go to my house." By then it was about 5:00am so we packed up and lay Ray in the front seat making him as comfortable as we could in hope he would be able to sleep on the trip home. Within minutes Ray fell asleep and rested with no problems for the next four hours.

Paul helped Ray back into his bed and asked him if he was hot, if so he'd take off his T-shirt Paul had given Ray a shirt that read, "Victory in Jesus" and Raymond loved it, so he said, "No, I want to wear it." We got Ray settled and all of us decided to get a little rest. About an hour later, Paul was heading for the bathroom when he saw Ray sliding out of his bed. He went in and pulled him back onto his pillow, noticing how limp he was. He also noticed how shallow his breathing was. "Ray, are you all right, buddy?" Ray quietly said, "Mom—love." Paul yelled for Pam and told her to quickly get me. I ran into his room and picked him up under his shoulders, holding his head and yelling, "Ray—Raymond," as though he were a child doing something wrong, and wasn't listening to his mother! I repeated myself in a fearful tone when I realized my son had stopped breathing. I shook him, still yelling his name, when suddenly, I felt his last two breaths blow into my face, lifting my hair. The good, the sick and the end—my son was gone! It was over.

Numb, I laid him down, looked at Paul and Pam and left the room. Not knowing what I was doing, I went to the phone and called the dialysis center to tell them. I think I thought that they could help him. They just told me that they would call the life squad for me to just hang up the phone and wait. They were there in just a few minutes but it felt like an eternity. They chased me out of the bedroom as they proceeded to try to revive him. I found myself praying that God was going to bring him back to life. Suddenly, I heard a voice, not verbally, but silently say, "No, Yvonne, you have to let him go now—he is at peace—he is in no pain."

By that time, they were bringing Ray out on a stretcher in front of me and I just looked at him, like he was peacefully sleeping and I said, "Yes Lord, I have to let go—bring him "HOME" to you Lord—take care of my baby." Paul and Pam, along with my Haitian friend and neighbor, Jeannie, were by my side trying to give me strength and comforting words as they took Ray out of the house. I was in a state of shock but I can remember it as though it were yesterday. I felt I was on the outside looking in, watching a movie in slow motion. I suddenly felt a peace, like I had never felt before and have never felt since. The Holy Spirit gave me strength I needed to face the most horrific pain I would ever endure.

I called my daughter, Lisa, and my youngest son, Joedy, and told them it was over. I remember saying their brother had just gone to be with the Lord. I then asked them to call Gary, my eldest son in California.

When the kids arrived at the house, they called my preacher and was told, he was in the hospital visiting the sick. It was the same hospital where they had taken Ray so we left to go make arrangements for Ray's body, and for all of us to say our final goodbyes. It was without a doubt the hardest thing any of us had to do, yet it is so necessary to put a finalization on this death. I told him how much I loved him and would miss him but I was happy he was free of pain and in the arms of Jesus, and one day I would join him there.

I remember Lisa saying something about his feet—like there will never be anybody with the same flat feet, fat toes, like his. (On January 19th she was proven wrong, when her beautiful daughter, Allyssa, was born, and yes, she has Raymond's feet. What a sense of humor our Lord has, I thought.)

While in the waiting room, a hospital attendant came out to ask me if Ray was an organ donor. We had never discussed it but I knew that Ray was such a giver in life, I had no doubt that he would give whatever was usable from his poor battered dialysized body. Months later, I received a beautiful letter saying they were able to use his eyes and because of Raymond, someone could now see. How great, I thought. Ray had warm, smiling eyes and I could just vision someone else with those same eyes, which made me feel so warm inside—through the window of their soul—their eyes are now my son's. I found myself looking at strangers eyes and wondering — could they be Ray's?

The rest of the day was filled with contacting family and close friends and deciding about the funeral. We had decided to have Ray cremated and took care of the church arrangements. I tried to rest but my mind wouldn't stop running so I wrote the poems God had given me, on the following pages, which I would read at the service. I just kept thinking, it's over, it's over. Trying to be happy for Ray, yet my heart wouldn't stop breaking. How will I get through this, Lord? Please give me the strength.

I dreaded having Ray's service. Lisa had made the arrangements with her preacher and Pam had made copies of the flyers about Raymond and the poems I had written. Every one else did their part. I did great just to get myself dressed. I wore a black and white polka-dot dress, which Raymond loved on me. We arrived early to set Ray's pictures and poems on a table for easy access for the guests, and soon greeted the early arrivals.

Since I had Ray cremated, we had no casket. I hate seeing anyone in a casket, which was one of reasons I had him cremated. My son-in-law, Mario, videotaped the whole ceremony, at my request. Some find this strange, but I am very glad we did it I was in such a state of shock, I didn't remember much of it and when I felt I could handle it, I watched it, crying tears of joy and pain. I also was able to send it to my relatives and those who requested it because they lived out of state.

One of Ray's friends said it best when he said, "Ray didn't have much, but he gave us all that he did have. He gave us laughter, something money can't buy. He was always so funny. Whenever I was down, Ray could still make me laugh. I loved him and will miss him very much." What a great thing to say about my son. It was also very true. Ray was a funny, funny kid. He often got into trouble in school but it gained him a lot of friends. He was also a giving, caring person who'd give you the shirt off his back. This was evident, looking over the filled room of teary-eyed guest.

One of the songs chosen to play at the ceremony was called, "If You Could See Me Now." That song gave me great peace as it said, "I'm running streets of gold, no longer in pain—if you could see me now you wouldn't want to see me leave this place." WOW! That song hit me hard! I closed my eyes and with tears streaming down my face, I envisioned Ray running—something he hadn't been able to do in a long time. He was laughing—no longer in pain—and he loved it! How awesome it was! It gave me the peace I desperately needed. Through the years, I still use this vision when I have my "Ray" days. When I miss him extra much and feel like I can't breathe. I think about him playing with all the wild animals, like the lions, tigers, elephants, etc., as I know how much Ray loves animals. I often look at the pictures of Ray with mom and my sisters, right before he died, to remind me how sick he looked and think how many times he would say, "I'm dying, mom, I'm dying," in a scared little boy voice. It broke my heart and I never knew what to say except, "I know honey, but you'll be all right. You'll be with Jesus and you won't have any more pain."

I feel like I should have hugged and kissed him more and told him I love you more, but I'm sure we all feel like that after our child is gone. I sometimes will say, "Jesus, please hug my little boy and tell him I love and miss him, but I'm so happy he suffers no more." I know He will, as I feel a big pressure lift from me—thank you, Jesus.

If you have lost your child through illness, remember they suffer no more and be happy for them. Do as I do, "vision" him (or her) running in those streets of gold, free of pain and hear their voice say, "Mom, be happy for me as I am here with Jesus." Hear them say, "I am getting our mansion ready for when we are together again." Trust me, it brings you peace.

Oh! Lord, I pray unto Thee, for I fear for my son, for his soul is wandering and searching ... he's unknown of Thy great love and power. Cast away the devil, I fear within him and show him the way to find eternal happiness and peace ... on this Your earth and in Your heavenly kingdom.

Sweet Loving Jesus, I love you so much and ask now of Thy help. Come into my child's body and let him do what pleases You ... Be his conscious ... and whisper NAY to wrongs and YEH to rights ... Be his heart ... and beat out love for all... Be his lips ... speaking out for the Lord ... Be his ears ... closing them to filth and opening them to the "WORD" of the Lord ... Be his eyes ... seeing the beauty you have given to all of us on this earth, out of Your love ... Be his mind ... thinking only good thoughts and behavior ... and be his strength ... to stand up for his Lord and Saviour ... and to rebel against Satan ....

Thank you Sweet Jesus ...
I love you ...
Amen...

Your daughter,
Yvonne

The Lord Writes With Crooked Letters

Often we don't understand
   why things in life must be
Our hearts are too heavy, too bitter
   to know God's meaning, you see

But, I learned, at an early age
   to accept God's Holy will
For He is wiser than I,
   this my parents deeply instilled

It's so hard to lose a loved one
   especially when it's your child
You think of the yesteryears
   you see his beautiful smile

I think of the many things
   Raymond did throughout the years
From the day he was born
   he brought me many tears

But he also gave me laughter
   as he did for all of you
Ray just had a way
   of bringing the sunshine through

Raymond REALLY loved people
   and he always wanted to give
He loved to boogey and party
   that's the way he lived

But all that so called living
   gave him an early death
He lived in pain for two years
   until he took his final breath

One might say, but why?
   God could've made him well
But if Ray started partying again,
   he might've gone to hell!

So God in all his wisdom
   knew what was best
He claimed Jesus as his Saviour
   before he was put to rest

Ray now walks with the Lord
   and sings with the angels too
Why he's probably up there partying
   doing the boog-a-lou

Once again he is standing
   his body is made whole
He is no longer in pain
   walking the streets of gold

I will miss my Ray-Ray
   but I thank God with all my heart
He came to know the Lord
   before from us, he part

For now he lives forever
   in a better place than you or I
Someday we will unite again
   in God's mansion in the sky

Until that day does come
  never will we forget
Ray's shinning personality
  his crazy kind of wit

We will all miss Ray-Ray,
  or whatever you called him
Uncle Buck, Big Daddy, Boy Roy
  his nickname of love from within

So when you feel those hot rays
  coming from the sun,
That's probably Ray-Ray
  just having fun

And if you look up at night,
  and look really far
That's my rascal Ray-Ray
  swinging from the star!

Where Is That Little Boy

Where is that little boy
  that I once knew
The one who made me smile
  when I was feeling blue

Where is that little boy
  a flower he'd bring each day
As he walked home from school
  he picked along the way

Where is that little boy
  who was so thoughtful of me
Helping in everyway
  always trying to please

Where is that little boy
  who use to pray to God
He got down on his knees
  with his head nod

He knew that God answers prayer
  just ask — that's all he'd do
What happened to that little boy
  oh, mom misses you

That little boy has grown
  now he is a man
He is always in a hurry
  I beg for his helping hand

He seldom prays to God
   does he know He's even there?
Does he think how Christ suffered
   because for us He cares

My little boy has changed so much
   for him I truly fear
Tragedy is in his life ...
   I fear the end is near

There is nothing a mother can do
   although it breaks her heart
She prays for lots of angels ...
   to protect each day as he starts

I've lost one son through death
   often it feels like it's two
I miss my little boy ...
   I'm sure that God does too ...

My Special Child

Hallelujah! Hallelujah!
  he suffers no pain
The Almighty Hand of the Lord
  has beckoned him to his Reign

It's so hard to let go
  of someone that we love
We know he is suffering
  and he must go to God above

For only then, will the pain stop
  his body will be whole again
It is his family who now suffer
  and all his many friends

Raymond was so very special
  from his day of birth
All the money in the world
  couldn't buy this child's worth

From the day that Ray was born
  he was anemic from the start
He's spit up every bottle
  it would just break my heart!

Pain was very familiar to Ray
  as he struggled through the years
Taking abuse from everyone
  specially his family dears

He was teased by family and friends
   for being overweight
He was screamed at constantly
   for the bed wetting that I'd hate

For this dear Ray-Ray
   we all apologize
Please forgive us honey,
   as you watch from the sky

Raymond was my rotten angel
   always into a mess
Oh how I prayed to God
   please God — Ray bless!

Ray's drinking and partying
   put him in an early grave
But we all make mistakes
   his took him away

Raymond loved to boogey
   he would dance 'til he dropped
He would be soaking wet
   from his feet to his top

Raymond really loved people
   he tried so hard to please
If you were his friend
   you were lucky as could be

With some who knew him
   it was a love-hate affair
Ray would mess up
   and get kicked out of somewhere

But he could call or go back
   an apologize to everyone
"I guess I got carried away
   having too much fun."

Everyone always forgave him
   you just couldn't stay mad at him
To know him was to love him
   he was really a friend

Ray and I had many a battle
   but he was so special to me
Down deep, I felt his hurt
   it was obvious to see

Especially in these past two years
   he suffered so very much
His arthritis was so severe
   he yelled if you just touched

Each day as I watched him
   my heart would just break
Dear God, I love him
   please home to heaven — please take

God has answered my prayers
Ray is now at peace
His pain is no longer
Satan has been released

Ray claimed Jesus Christ
   as his Saviour and Lord
So I know he's with the one
   he deeply loved and adored

He battled with Satan
  for so many many years
But down deep Ray knew
  it was God he most feared

In the end, Almighty God conquered
  Raymond lifted his hand in praise
He said, "I love you Jesus"
  O Glorious days!

So now we all must suffer
  for we will miss him so
But let us all rejoice
  for he's with our God, we know

We will miss you my special child
  but never will we forget
All the pleasures you gave to us
  all your silly kind of wit

Someday we will unite
  Ray will meet us there
He'll greet us at those Pearly Gate
  there'll be rejoicing everywhere

You are still my special child,
  Ray you are my angel in the sky
I know you'll watch over us
  I know you'll be close by

Love you Ray-Ray,
Mom, Loved Ones and Friends

Corinthians 5:8 *We are confident, I say, and willing rather to be absent from the body and to be present with the Lord.*

Remember Your Other Kids

About a year after Ray's death, my daughter, Lisa, gave me a wake-up call. I don't remember exactly what happened but I know she wanted me to go with her somewhere and as usual I rejected, saying, "I didn't feel like it." "Mom, I know you miss Raymond, as we all do but it's time you remember you have other kids too," she said angrily. "I know I have other kids but you have no idea the pain I am going through and I pray you never do," I answered. "Mom, I loved Ray and I was very close to him as you know and I still cry as I miss him terribly, but I have to go on in life for the sake of my kids and husband. You, too, have to get on with your life. Every time I ask you to do something, or Joedy asks you, you say, 'I don't feel like it.' "I'm sorry but it's time you joined the living."

I was terribly hurt by what she said, but thought she just doesn't know what I'm going through. Not long after this incident, I was watching one of my favorite shows, "*Oprah*," when I believe God sent me the message. A woman who had lost her child was telling the same type of story that happened with her kids. She reacted the same way I did at first, but after thinking about it, she knew they were right. She had been neglecting her other kids in the same manner as I. That show really hit me. I felt it was sent to me from God, telling me how wrong I had been. I started crying. I guess they were tears of joy and pain for seeing the realism and for thinking how I had been hurting my children. I called Lisa to tell her that I was sorry and I now understood where she was coming from. I promised to do my best to change my ways but to be patient with me.

I was grateful to God for I felt His hand was in this eye-opener. I was so thankful for this lady who shared her story which helped me and I'm sure many others who were like her and me in their time of pain.

My love and gratitude to Oprah Winfrey for opening her heart through all of her shows, to help those lost souls and in just one show, get that—ahha or B-I-N-G-O feeling, as she would say. She is a beautiful human being, of which I'm sure God is so well pleased with her doing His work on this earth. She is definitely an "Angel" in many ways to many, many, people. Her topics have touched me as well as numerous people in need of a loving touch. I have a deep admiration and love for 'Oprah,' God's Creation. I say with the utmost honesty, thank you Oprah for blessing me.

I now tell those who have lost a child not to forget the kids that are still alive. Of course, I don't tell them as soon as their tragedy happens, but I give them time to grieve. We have a way of completely shutting down the rest of the world and we could care less about anyone or anything else. I didn't realize I was doing this, especially to my kids, but when I realized it, it really saddened me to think how much I was hurting them.

Thanks to my wake-up call from Lisa, God, and a stranger and Oprah, I started living among the living.

My Special Child
GARY

Why wasn't I your "special child?"
   my daughter said to me
I found this question familiar
   as I thought that way, you see

When I was a young girl
   I too was jealous of sis,
I thought, "She's more special,"
   as Mom gave her a hug and a kiss

It wasn't until years later
   I had children of my own
Each one is entirely different
   none of them are clones

You love them all very much,
   each in a "special" way
I guess the reason being,
   God molded them from different clay

I thought about this question
   so I'm using my God-given gift
To explain why each are special,
   how you all give me a lift

Gary is my "special child"
   because he was first born
I was still a child myself
   my teenage years were torn

I clung to him for security
  he was the only happiness,
I knew Without this bundle of joy,
  I didn't know what I'd do

I thought he was my "angel"
  as all mothers do of their first
They don't want to know different
  for their heart might burst

He was a straight "A" student
  which made me so proud
Especially being a single parent
  I was walking on a cloud

He was so independent
  never asking me for much
He'd work hard as a child
  bought his own clothes and such

Being the oldest child
  he had his hands full
Taking care of brother and sister
  while I worked or acted a fool

I knew he wasn't perfect
  but I knew he tried
Always trying to please me
  or comfort me when I cried

Now he's grown into a man
  a teacher he's become
Making his mother proud
  of her Number 1 son!

But no matter what he has chosen
    to do with his life
To live the life of a bachelor
    or have lots of kids and a wife

What really matters to mom
    is the WAY you live, my son
It's what you do for Christ
    that counts when you are done

For knowing that someday,
    we will be together again
For all eternity —
    because we lived free of sin

That's what a mother prays for
    from the day of your birth
For all the riches on this earth
    don't compare to Heaven's worth

I love you dear, Gary
    as a son, you've been the best
Keep your eyes on the Lord
    and he will do the rest!!

Just Because

In case I haven't told you lately
  (I truly hope I did)
I love you very much
  my Number #1 kid

Although you've been a man
  for many many years
To me, you're still my baby
  giving me joy and tears

It seems like only yesterday
  I rocked you on my knee
Singing, "Two little blue birds
  sitting in a tree"

It wasn't so easy then
  raising you little ones
We had our problems ...
  but we also had our fun

Although my walk with Christ
  wasn't as strong as should've been
Christ was always there for me ...
  just like a good friend

As I look back on those days
  many things I would've changed
Spend more time with my kids ...
  from partying I'd refrain

One thing we can't change
   the way we lived in the past
Now I've found my joy
   with Christ it will last

One thing I don't regret
   is having my four babies
Although I love you all at times
   you drove me crazy

I thought my heart would break
   when you moved away
Out to California ...
   with your dad to stay

I want you to know, Gary
   I missed you my son
I prayed for angels to protect
   with each rising sun

I still pray that angels
   protect you night and day
And that you let God ...
   direct your path's way

And yes, I still miss you
   but you know what they say..
Absence makes the heart fonder
   I love you more each day

I'm also very happy
   you have Rita in your life
I love her like a daughter
   hopefully someday your wife

I wrote this, "JUST BECAUSE"
  not for any occasion, my son
"JUST BECAUSE" I love you
  and still my Number #1 ...

My Special Child
RAYMOND

Raymond is my "special child"
  for many reasons, you see
He was always into trouble
  rebellious as could be

From the time I was in labor
  he was the hardest to bare
He was sick his day of birth
  and it didn't stop there

Ray needed special caring
  because he was sick, you see
I spent endless hours
  just trying he, to feed

He'd throw up every bottle
  ten baths a day he had
He was so thin and helpless
  he made my heart sad

I knew then he was special
  he'd always need special care
He proved me right —
  in hospitals everywhere!!

His accidents were un-ending
  the doctors all knew him by name
If child abuse was known
  I would've been blamed

Because of his "unreasonable" wetting
  he took abuse from everyone
Scaring him mentally
  when he should've been having fun

No one truly realized
  the hell he was going through
Not even his mother
  knew what to do

Now he is "Very Special"
  this poem he never read
For he is at peace now
  he's in his final bed

I miss his beautiful smile
  the funny things he'd do
Saying, "Mom, you're the best,"
  or saying, "I love you."

But I thank God daily
  for my Ray suffers no more
Someday he will meet me
  when I go to Heaven's door

One thing is for certain
  he was very "special" to me
He needed me so much more
  than the other three

I think he's my guardian angel
  as he watches me from above
As always, still by my side,
  my "Special Angel Love!"

My Special Child
ALICIA

Alicia is my "Special Child,"
  because she is my only girl
Oh what a beauty she was
  with her brown little curls

I was so excited
  when God sent her my way
I had a live doll baby
  to "dress" up every day

I loved buying her dresses
  and dollies for her to play
I thanked God sincerely
  every night and day

Of course with two brothers
  a tomboy she became
Instead of calling her Alicia
  Sissy became her name

That was familiar to me
  I was a tomboy too
I was also called Sissy
  until I was twenty-two

My daughter was my "special child"
  she gave back my youth to me
As I watched her grow
  it was like watching me, you see

But she gave me more fear
   than any of my boys
Especially as she got older
   looking at boys instead of toys

Maybe I didn't handle my fear
   the way that I should
There are things that I'd change
   if only that I could

But since we can't go back in time
   there's something I can do
Tell my "special daughter,"
   how proud I am of you

You've become a beautiful lady
   on the inside and out
Always there to help me
   on you I can count

Studying hard to become a nurse
   this achievement made me proud
"My daughter is a nurse!"
   I boast Very Loud!!

You also are a loving wife
   to a man who is great
A good mother to Justin and Shaun
   motherhood is your fate

What makes me feel most proud
   is to see you walk with Christ
This gives a mother peace of heart
   my fears have taken flight

Someday, I pray Lisa
   that you have a daughter too
The words can not explain
   how much they mean to you

So, if I haven't told you
   you hold a "special" place in my heart
Only between a mother and daughter
   can this feeling take part

To me you will always be
   that little girl I love
With those cute little dimples
   sent from God above!!

Joedy Is My Special Child

Joedy is my "SPECIAL CHILD"
   for many reasons too
He came to me out of prayer
   when feeling alone and blue

I prayed in earnest nightly
   "Dear God send me a "LOVE"
God in all His Wisdom —
   sent a child from above

I didn't need another child
   it was hard raising my three
I wanted to be loved by a man
   and to help with my family

Thoughts of adoption haunted me
   even abortion too
"Dear God," I shouted,
   "I'm so depressed — confused!

But God knew that a child's love
   was exactly what I did need
For that love is unconditional
   and will last for eternity

From the very first moment
   I held my baby boy
I knew I made the right decision
   he gave me unbelievable joy

He was ten years younger —
   than my last child born
He was loved by us all —
   he was truly adorn

He got more attention
   but not just from me
His older brothers and sister
   thought he was the greatest, you see

As the years flew by
   he proved them right
He was "SUNSHINE ON MY SHOULDER"
   through the day and night

Joedy is my "Special Child"
   because he's thoughtful in many ways
Like picking Mommy a flower —
   walking home from school each day

Earning his own money
   before the age of ten
Offering it to help his Mommy
   or just for him to spend

Always giving of himself—
   anyway he can
He hasn't changed in that way —
   my "SPECIAL LITTLE MAN"

Every day I thank my Lord
   for this special boy
He still gives Mommy flowers
   and blesses me with joy

I especially thank my Lord
    for my "Special Little Gift"
A child's love — not a man
    who's given my life a lift

Joedy is my "SPECIAL CHILD"
    because he is truly God's gift of "LOVE"
When I had a hurting, empty heart
    He filled it with a child — from above ...

                    Thank you God for all of my
                    "SPECIAL CHILDREN" ...

A Parent's Prayer

Dear Heavenly Father...Up above
Watch and protect these children we love

Keep them safe...both night and day
In their work, sleep and play

Teach them to love you...as we their parents do
For we know Lord they were blessed on us by you

I wrote this poem when I was pregnant with my first
child...almost forty years ago. I changed it from child to
children when I had Ray, my second child—then Lisa and
Joedy. I still pray this every day for my kids and now for
their kids.

After each birth of my children, I changed the singular to the plural, such as, he to they, etc. I pray it in the evening and in the morning for all my kids and I include my grandchildren. I truly believed that God has honored that prayer and has kept my children safe for all these years. I know there were plenty of times they could have been injured in car accidents and other ways, and I thank God none of them have been harmed in any way.

Yes, I hear you readers, loud and clear. I had a son who died. Where was God's protection then? He was there carrying him through his pain. I had Ray for thirty-one years and in those years, Ray was always into something from the time he was born. I have no doubt if the heavenly angels had not been protecting him, I wouldn't have had him near that long.

One time Ray was playing with his friends and got hit in the eye with a rock. He came into the house screaming and I thought I would pass out. His eye was pouring blood. I was talking to mom and quickly said, "I got to go and take Ray to the Emergency Room again." The eye specialist said he feared Ray would lose his eye but they would know for sure in about a week. They had both eyes covered (so not to strain the good eye) and was going to keep him there in order to keep him still until they had the results by next week.

The next day, I went in early to see him and he said, "Mommy, my eye is going to be okay because when I said my prayers last night, Jesus told me it would be." Patronizing my sick son, I said, "I know, honey, it will be fine." (If only we adults had the faith of a child, we too would see more miracles!) When the doctor came in, Ray told him what he had told me and like me, he said, "Well, we will know in about a week, but let's see how it looks today." He took off the bandage and as doctors will say,

"Hummm," followed by another inquisitive, "Hummm," checked it again, looked at me—checked his eye again, and mumbled, "How strange," "What's wrong?" I asked nervously. "Nothing, that's what I don't understand. His eye looks like there is no damage—at all."

He then had more tests done to see what was going on. He came back to the room with the same bewildering look and said, "Well, I don't understand but the tests all say his eye is fine." "I thought it would be at least a week," I said to him. "So did I, as that is the usual time of healing if it does heal, and to be honest, I thought his eyesight was gone in that eye." Ray said, "See Doc, I told you, Jesus healed my eye. "Ray," the doctor said, "I believe you are right." He looked at me and said, "I think your son is right I believe we just saw a miracle happen—there is no other answer!"

I thought it was strange that Ray's doctor said that he had to be a miracle, especially back in that time. You never heard of a doctor giving God the credit even if they knew it was true. I have heard of doctors saying today that there is healing in the power of prayer and have seen some doctors and nurses pray with their staff before surgery and with families.

Anyhow, the doctor kept Ray there overnight and released him the next day with the bandages off.

The word spread fast throughout the hospital about the miracle on the six year old. To Ray, it was just something Jesus said He would do—and He did it! As for me, it took me back to my youth, to when I would have believed it was possible and it should have been I who asked Jesus for that miracle. I couldn't thank Jesus enough for loving my son enough to give back his eyesight.

As I write this, it has just come to me, that the only organ that they could use of Ray's, after his death, was his eyes. Everything else was too badly damaged from the years of dialysis, which is strange, because so many people's eyes are affected by the treatment. When Jesus heals you, He heals you!

Raymond had so many accidents when he was young that we could go into any hospital, day or night, for treatment and they all knew him by his first name. It's a good thing that child abuse wasn't so big back then or I know I would've been accused. Ray was just, let's say, adventurous. He was an accident waiting to happen. I could write a book (someday, I may) on the things he did and all the accidents he had in his short life. What I do know is that I don't honestly believe Ray would have lived as long as he did without the protection of God and His angels throughout his many calamities.

The Rose

Before the death of my son, Raymond, I looked at the "Rose" as just a beautiful flower, which I, like most, enjoyed receiving from a loved one. Now, the rose has a much more profound meaning because whenever Ray would give me a card, he would draw me a rose. Ray was far from being an artist but his rose was always the same style and was very pretty. Most importantly, it came from his heart, so it always had great meaning but even more so after his death.

Every time I see a rose, I think of my Ray-Ray. I started putting a copy of his rose on the poems which I wrote for the parents whose child had died.

After God sent me Ray's rose from heaven, I guess I need to give an explanation for that strange statement before I continue.

I had asked for prayers in my Bible class for a family which I knew, that had a son who recently died. This was the second son to die for Jeanie, the mother. I had known her and the family for years and I knew how she was struggling to get through this terrible tragedy. I also knew that none of the family were Christians, therefore, they didn't know the love and strength of God was just waiting there for them. All they had to do was ask for His help.

Two weeks later a man who had lost his son, came up to me and handed me a poem. More importantly, he had also handed me a letter written to Jeanie and her family.

Ironically, this man use to drink in a bar that Jeanie owned. He had known her and the family for twenty years. He wrote in the letter that he give up drinking when he came to the Lord and if it had not been for God, he doesn't think his wife nor him could have gotten through the worst pain in their lives; that being, losing their son. (a poem of his son is included in this book)

After telling him, I would be happy to give the letter to them, I started to sit down when I spilled my coffee on the letter, I quickly tried to dry it before it ruined what he had written. I was speechless as I looked at the paper, before my eyes appeared a rose—not just any rose, it was shaped like my Ray-Ray's! Every hair on my body stood up.

"Oh, my gosh, look at this!" I said to the lady next to me. "What does this look like?" I asked showing her the stain. "A rose," she calmly said, not knowing why I was so excited. Everyone I showed it to quickly responded the same way. Thank God, I made copies of it as I somehow lost the original one. (I am still praying I find it) After I'd tell everyone that it was from a coffee spill, they were just as stunned as I was. I truly felt God was letting them know that their sons were in Heaven with my Ray-Ray.

I am still amazed every time I look at that rose from God—not because God could do that, but because He loves me enough to take the time to do that for me and the other two families who lost their sons.

Yes, I definitely look at the rose in a very different and unique way since I received my Miracle Rose from God.

Since that time, I have seen and heard numerous ways the rose has affected people. Not long ago, I kept smelling roses in my living room but I didn't have real roses, only silk arrangements which I made. For several days, I kept smelling this aroma. I mentioned it to a friend and she said, "You must have angels in your house." I had never heard of that before, but she wasn't the only one who told me that. Shortly after that I saw a show on T.V. (I think it was on It's A Miracle) which said the same thing as my friend.

A few months later, A Christian lady friend was at my house and while we were praying, began to giggle. I continued to pray but asked her when I was finished, what as so funny? She said she opened her eyes at one point because she sensed someone was with us, and she saw an angel over my shoulder. I sense an angel around me all the time, but so far I haven't seen any, other than the many, many, miniature ones I have collected throughout my house.

Nonetheless, I feel that one day God is going to allow me to see one, so I thank Him now for that honor.

A similar incident occurred while I was in Ohio visiting my family. Linda, the head of Master's Touch Ministry was praying over me when she suddenly giggled in the midst of the prayer. She told me later that she had seen an angel sitting over my shoulder.

I have no doubt God gives us these beautiful creatures to watch over us, but I had never heard of the scent of roses accompanying them.

So, if you suddenly smell roses in your house and you have none around, just say, "Hello, Angel!" Since hearing this, I have others tell me that they smelled the scent of roses in their house after the death of a loved one, so don't freak if you do. It is just God sending you a little extra strength in the shape of an angel.

When I thought about putting the stories of the rose into this book. I thought of a story I had seen on T.V. but couldn't remember all the details about it. So like I always do, I asked God to help me to remember or to reveal it to me again. Not long afterwards, I was awakened from a sound sleep with the words, "A Rose is a Rose is a Rose." I laid there for a second before I realized I wasn't dreaming, but was hearing it from my T.V. which I had left on. I rolled over to see what I heard and it was the program Beyond Chance which was telling the story I asked God to reveal to me.

It was about the faith of a mother whose son in his early twenties, was critically injured in a car accident with no hope of recovery, (According to his physicians.)

If by a slight chance that he did live, they said he would never be able to walk, talk or do anything for himself. In other words, they said he would be in a vegetative state. Being a Christian, his mother refused to accept this fate and called upon the Greatest Physician of all, Jesus Christ. If He could give eye sight to the blind, hearing to the deaf, raise the dead to life, no doubt He could and would save her son from this "life" of Hell.

After months of endless prayers, someone told her about a nun that healed people when she was alive. They also knew of miracles that took place after her death. She was known as "The Little Rose." It was said that when she healed someone the scent of roses could be smelled.

Being a Christian, she knew to pray directly to God, Jesus, or the Holy Spirit, but she didn't pray to the nun. Up to now, her son was still in the hospital in a comatose state, unable to do or say a word. She asked God if He would allow the nun to give her a sign that her son was going to be healed. The sign she asked for was a rose.

After her prayer, she and her daughter were pulling into the hospital parking lot, when she yelled to her daughter, "Back up," and yelled something about a rose. Her daughter knew nothing of her prayer or of the nun, so she had no idea what her mother was yelling about, but she stopped and backed up. It was the dead of winter with a blanket of snow and in the midst of that, was sticking out one beautiful red rose! "Look!" yelled the mother. "A rose?" her daughter said in complete disbelief. "That is the answer to my prayer," telling her daughter about the rose.

As they hurried into the hospital, they saw their second miracle. Walking toward them on crutches was her son! "Hi, mom." He said and then greeted his sister. They were in tears of joy and shock! Not only had he learned how to walk and talk, he lives a completely normal life today. What an awesome God we serve!

Of course, I layed there and watched the entire show with tears streaming down my face and praising God. Then I thanked God for waking me up to answer my prayer and I fell back into my peaceful sleep.

No doubt, the rose is the favorite flower when wanting to show your affection to loved ones. My youngest son, Joedy, has had a great love of flowers ever since he was six years old. Everyday on his walk home from the school bus, he would stop at our neighbor's and pick me one flower. He'd come running into the house with that flower behind his back and say, "I got you a surprise, mommy." Everyday, I would act surprised as I hugged my little one for this thoughtful way of saying, I love you.

Joe never outgrew his love for God's beautiful creations. When he got a little older, he'd spend some weekends at my friend Jill's house. Her husband, Tim, was the caretaker of a mansion in Palm Beach. They had their own green house and Joe always came home with a bouquet of the largest, most beautiful multi-colored roses, that I had ever seen. It was no surprise to me that within a few years, Joe became the neighborhood caretaker.

One by one, the yards looked like they had been manicured. He was only nine when he started and within six to seven years, he was hired to do so many he could hardly keep up, so with the money he had saved, he started his own yard business. He eventually was hired where his friend Tim worked in Palm Beach.

Now at the age of twenty-nine, he still works for Palm Beachers and still brings his mom a beautiful rose from time to time. Seldom can I walk into his house without seeing a bouquet of roses. The smell of roses is always in his home. I'm sure some of that aroma is from the angels which surround him. Thank you God!

On a recent trip to Ohio to visit my family, I stayed at my brother Paul's and Pam's house a few nights and I had a very strange experience the first night I slept there. The bedroom was completely dark except for a small red light which glowed from the alarm clock next to my bed. As usual I had to go to the bathroom sometime in the early hours and when I got back into the bed, I noticed a shadow on the ceiling, directly over my bed—and only over my bed. As I said, it was pitch black in that room, thus I couldn't figure out how a shadow could show. The shadow seemed to be a tree branch with roses on it. I got out of the bed and turned on the overhead light to see what was causing the shadow. I could see absolutely nothing that would cause this image. I even looked out of the blind (which was pulled down) to see if there was a rose bush outside of the window, but there wasn't. I turned out the light and just laid there staring at the ceiling being a little frightened as if something was going to suddenly happen. But what? I didn't know. I then asked God what as He trying to tell me.

I don't know how long I laid there before I turned over to my right side and suddenly I could smell roses. I sniffed the sheets and the smell was stronger. The story of the rose aroma and the angels surrounding came to mind. "I guess you are just telling me I have angels with me in their room," I said to the Lord, and I quickly fell back into the best sleep I had in a long time.

The next morning I asked Pam if she had powdered or sprayed the sheets that may be causing them to smell like roses. "No," she said, asking "Why?" I told her about the shadow on the ceiling and the smell of roses on the sheets. I then told her that the smell of roses means that angels are present. Paul and Pam's house is surrounded with the little statues of angels (as is mine) and she also has artificial roses all over their house. She said, "I know we have angels (real ones) since everyone who comes here says they feel or sense them in our house."

The following night another shadow appeared. This time, it looked like a huge tree—not just a branch. There were no roses on it like the night before—just a huge tree—like the ones in Ohio—not like the palm trees in Florida which I am use to seeing. When I got back from the bathroom, I looked out the window and noticed there was a large tree similar to the one on the ceiling, but there was no way it was the shadow in my room. I turned out the light and noticed that the tree looked like a big bush now—and it went from over my bed to the left far corner—like a funnel. It dawned on me that it resembled a tornado! "Oh, my gosh!" I said. "Lord are you trying to warn me about a storm?" I just laid there and prayed for Angels to protect us from any storm that might be heading our way.

The very next day, there were storms and tornadoes in the vicinity but none of them hit in the area where I was, but very close. I have no doubt, the Lord showed me this. I shared the experience with my family the next morning.

The Greatest of Pain

Why did he have to die!!??
   I shouted through my tears
He was my little boy
   so young...so young, in years

He loved you, Lord Jesus
   he lived his life for you!!
He was washed in your blood
   this pain help me through!!

Then suddenly, I heard a voice
   from down deep within,
I felt God's arms around me
   felt peace, that once freed me of sin

I did not forsake you,
   nor did I your child
I was with him in the storm
   I carried him all the while

Bryan now is here with Me
   here where he is safe
I feared for Bryans' soul
   as satan he did face

A free will, I have given
   to each one of you,
To make your own decisions
   in everything you do

Bryan made the wrong choice
   when he left your loving home
Living with troubled kids
   in satan's world they roamed

My blood was upon him
   as he faced the evil one
I took him "HOME" quickly
   because he's also my son

I know your heart is breaking
   but it could've been worse
If he had chosen satans' way
   hell could've been his curse

I knew what was best for HIM
   and what I had to do
Because of my decision
   he'll spend eternity with you

I know there is no greater pain
   for this I felt too
As I watched My Son, Jesus die
   out of love for all of you

I will help you through the pain
   as the days go by
Just come to me in prayer
   I will comfort your cry's

Donna-My Earthly and Heavenly Angels

The greatest day in your life
  and in your husbands' too
Was when your first baby—
  was sent from God to you

A beautiful baby girl
  Donna she would be named
Dreaming about her future
  and what would be her fame

You and Vincent were so excited
  with prayers of more children to come
Your hearts were filled with joy
  with this adorable little one

Just three and a half years later
  both your hearts would break
When the hand of death
  little Donna would take

A drunk driver out of no where
  flipped your car through the air
Oh God! Not our Donna!
  This just isn't fair

It was Halloween—
  satans' night you know
He sends out his demons
  to kill innocent souls

But several miracles happened
   which showed God was there
Baby Michael was un-harmed
   He kept him in His care

The car was destroyed
   but you and Vince were OK
But your sweet baby Donna—
   went to Jesus to stay

That's been so many years ago Janie
   but the pain I know is there
No matter how short or long it's been
   your heart it still tears

God did bless you with 3 more kids
   after little Michael I mean
There was David, Joe and Marsha
   which you were grateful to He

But I know my dear friend
   no matter how many kids you birth
Never can you replace one
   they are our treasures worth

God blessed you with another Donna
   who became your neighbor and friend
A friendship lasting all these years
   from you both deep within

You became her "SPECIAL ANGEL"
   in many many ways
Helping with her children
   you need each other those days

Isn't our God AWESOME
  He wanted to ease your pain
So He gave you another daughter
  whose name was the same

You know as a Christian Janie
  we can see our children again
For they are in the arms of Jesus
  our Saviour and our Friend

For He is THE key to the KINGDOM
  the ONLY way to get in
We just accept Him as our Lord and Saviour
  who died for our sins

Oh what a GLORIOUS day Janie
  when your daughter welcomes you
Along with your love — Vince
  into God's Kingdom too

True Friends Are Treasures

True friends are a rarity
  one who's there for you
To help you through your problems
  make rainbows from the dew

When I was a little girl,
  I had a friend like this
His name was Bobby Lyons
  he, I'll deeply miss

Bobby wasn't just a friend,
  to me, he was my bro,
Everywhere that I went,
  Bob would also go

Every night at suppertime
  Bobby was also there
Sitting at the table
  waiting for his share

Each night before we'd go to sleep
  I would hear Bobby call
He was across from our bedroom window
  sitting in his hall

We would talk and laugh
  about the events that day
Until mom and dad would yell
  it's time to hit the hay

Bobby was a namesake
    for my REAL third brother
When it came to choosing names
    we would have no other

Even when I grew older
    Bobby was there for me
Offering a shoulder to cry on
    always there to please

Bobby would make me laugh
    even when I was blue
He always had a way,
    of bringing the sunshine through

Throughout the many years
    even though I moved away
Bob had a special place
    in my heart, he'd always stay

Bob's love for people was evident
    there were no strangers to him
Just give him five minutes
    you had a new friend

We will miss his beautiful smile
    that childish giggle, he had
The way he brightened the room
    when you were feeling sad

I'll remember all the good times
    when we as children played
Bob was my knight in shinning armor
    or maybe a cowboy that day

I'll never forget the time
   Bob was a cowboy,
He was shooting a gun
   only it wasn't a TOY!!

We found daddy's gun,
   in the upstairs where we played
We almost got a beaten,
   that fun-filled day

Kick-the-can was a favorite game
   and also hide-go-seek
Bobby was so funny —
   because he'd always peek!

I could write a book
   about this great friend
He was always there for you,
   through thick and thin

He loved his sisters and family
   Linda, his love of fourteen years
Jennifer was his pride and joy
   they were his special dears

Rocky," as he was affectionately called
   will be missed by family and friends
But never will we forget
   the love he gave from within

I thank God, he didn't suffer,
   from this terrible disease
Some have paid for years
   they live in misery

But God in all His Wisdom
   knew what was best
He took Bobby home
   with his parents, he now rest

Bob won't be lonely there
   he'll be with his brothers, too
James, Jacque and Donald
   will be waiting there for you

Linda

Linda was married to my brother, Joe, and she was truly a beautiful woman, inside and out. She had a son, Chris and with Joe, they had cute little Sue Ellen, who they both adored. The news of Linda's cancer shocked and saddened us all.

Whenever I went home to Ohio, I looked forward to our visits together. Linda and I were alike in many ways, because we both loved antiques and making crafts. She always took me to some great antique and thrift shops and then to a special little place for some delicious homemade food and mouth-watering pies! We shared our good and bad times and just enjoyed our time together. She was such a joy to be with and we loved sharing our love for Christ.

Brother Joe and Linda were in the church choir and it was a blessing to watch them as they praised the Lord with their voices. Linda was Joe's first true love and it was obvious how much he adored her.

When you hear the word cancer, you associate death with it, but now there is hope; especially if you catch it in the early stages. No doubt, Jesus, who is the greatest physician, can heal anyone of anything, but that doesn't always come about. Why God will heal one person and not the next is a mystery to me as it is to everyone else.

One might say, (and they did), why wouldn't God heal Linda since she was a good Christian and lived her life for Him? Only God knows the answer and we shouldn't ask why. I know that cancer is evil, thus it did not come from God. He choose not to heal her, I believe is because so much good has come from her death.

Joe is now in a healing ministry, which has healed many, in need of not just physical healing but even more importantly, their souls were set free of the disease. They in return dedicated their lives to Christ. His life consisted of serving the Lord before, but now he is completely dedicated to winning souls for Him. This is only one of the examples of the good that has come out of Linda's death. Needless to say, Joe didn't want to give up his beloved Linda when she died, but in all honesty, he came through it much better than I had expected. He gives all the glory to God, for without His strength, he knows he could have never gotten through the pain and might have turned back to his days of partying and forgotten the Lord, blaming Him as so many do.

Linda was here to see Chris get married and even made the wedding gown for the bride, Karen. I have heard some say too bad she wasn't here to see her first grandchild. I believe, she was allowed to see that child from above and she watches over all her loved ones.

When I got the call that Linda had gone back into the hospital because of a relapse, I had this gut feeling that it was the end. Two days later, I started writing her and Joe a letter at 7:00a.m. I felt eerie with each word I wrote like someone was watching me. I would actually look over my shoulder to see if there was someone there. After a couple of minutes, I knew it was Linda. She is here with me. She has already died! I was on my first page and I ended it quickly, saying Linda, give my love and kisses to my loved ones— you know who I mean. I meant my dad and Raymond who had both died. I knew in my heart she was already gone.

As soon as I signed "Love, Sis," the phone rang and it was my sister Donna. "Sis, she said,—"Yes, I know...Linda died," I said. "How did you know? Did someone call you?" "No, I feel her presence her." Then I explained about the letter and sensing her presence. Since my sister knew about my vision dreams and other experiences with the Lord, she knew it was true.

I sent that letter to Joe, along with the explanation. God gave me the words for her poem to send home to be read at her service. Joe said it was obvious the words were from God as I had written about things I didn't know had happened. I have no doubt they are the words of the Lord, because as I have stated before, I have to read it when I'm finished to see what I have written. I am only God's instrument to help ease the pain and hopefully win souls for His great Kingdom!

We all miss Linda deeply but her love for us and ours for her, will remain in our hearts until we see her again in Heaven; where I would bet she is now singing in God's Choir of Angels! Hallelujah!!!

Hush, Hush, Sweet Loved-Ones

Hush, Hush, sweet loved-ones cry not for me,
For it's only farewell — not goodbye, you see

Someday we'll be together in God's beautiful land
We'll walk his streets of gold, as we talk and hold hands

I'll still be with you, for I'm a part of each of you
I gave you life and love Chris — and my sweet daughter
Sue

My wonderful husband Joe, you were so good to me
Close your eyes, feel your heart — and there I'll always be

I was so proud of you Sunday, when you told Satan where to
    go!!!
You know he'll tempt you now — but you can beat him my
    darling Joe

I know it's hard to understand — only God can tell you why,
Just continue to do his work and I'll be by your side

God did tell me honey, that I was going away
I wanted to tell you, but the words I could not say

That's why I couldn't miss Sue's 16th birthday
I knew it was my last, on this earth anyway

I'll watch you every year Sue, as the candles out you blow,
I pray your walk with God will get stronger as you grow

Take good care of daddy Sue, he needs you there with him
Help him through his pain — we'll be together again

Chris, I'm so proud of you, I just want you to know
I asked God to live for your wedding. He let it be so

I cant wait to see my grandchild Oh! I'll watch from above
Kiss your lovely wife for me and give the baby my love

God did prepare me honey, that's why I had to say
Thank you, I love you — at Sue's party that day

I tried to tell my friend Linda, but she knew in her heart
She just didn't want to let go. She just couldn't part.

I love you Linda and Chester, take care of my great man
Always stay by his side — help whenever you can

I love you mom and dad, with my family, I was blessed
Always there for me — God truly gave me the best

Poem for Joe

God's ways are not like ours this we've learned is true
  But still the pain goes unexplained
  Where my Lord were you?

We stood in faith believing no doubts would we allow
  Expecting total victory, but instead only broken hearts
  And unanswered questions for now

Are we wrong for what we feel? Did we miss your
    will O'King?
  For never have I seen such faith
  To fail of hope to bring

But then I heard you say my child remember Calvary
  For that is where my son, your Lord cried
  My God, My God why has thou forsaken me?

Your High Priest my brother understand; abandonment
  And all the hurt it brings
And He forever intercedes for you and shall come
  With healing in His wings

So don't lose heart my friend, my brother
  He knows your loss is great
He's closer than He's ever been
  And is reaching for your hand to take

And not only Him but sister Linda
  Is smiling down on you
For she's so proud of this man she loves
  And she whispers, Joe, if you only knew!

It's been worth it all and I'd do it again
   For His glory is more than we can stand
More beautiful than you can imagine
   Thank you Joe my wonderful husband

I encourage you to be all that God created you to be
   I live forever in your heart
   And shall never be far from thee

I'll see ya soon cause He's coming back
   Please bring everyone with you
Keep praising his name, exalt Jesus
   I'm here because its Christ I knew

By inspiration of the SPIRIT
of the living GOD

Uncle Sonny

Rest now, Uncle Sonny,
　There's no more 'pain'
You're going to a better place
　Where God will reign…

He's bringing you home
　To the one, you love so
Your heart was breaking,
　This God did know..,

Your beloved wife, Carol,
　Had left your side,
Your life felt empty,
　As each day went by…

You fulfilled your wishes
　Now it was time to go
Your life was finished…
　On this land below

You were there for Missy
　To see her wed
She, deeply in love,
　You had nothing to dread…

You knew that now,
　You could go away
She had a new "keeper"
　She need not be afraid…

She would always miss you,
   But she would understand
You longed for her mother…
   Just to hold her hand…

God in all His wisdom,
   Showed "Sonny" another way
To fulfill his dreams
   Before his final day

He took Missy to Ohio
   To meet all of us there
Now she knows his family,
   For her, we love and care…

He was also blessed..
   After too many years,
He was re-united,
   With all his family dears

Uncle Bud, his older brother
   Oh, how he loved you,
Clara, he called "Mom",
   His sisters, Jean and Mary Lou

His nieces, Donna and Yvonne,
   Everyone thought were his sissy's
Are there for you whenever
   Just call on us, dear Missy…

That goes for all his nieces,
   His nephews and cousins too
We will keep you in our prayers,
   God will help you through…

To us, he was "big brother"
  How we loved him so
It was good to see him,
  Just to let him know…

Our memories of "Uncle Sonny"
  Put a smile upon our face
There were so many great times,
  Nothing can take their place…

Like twirling his baton,
  Leading the band at Catholic High
He'd throw it up so far,
  We couldn't see it in the sky…

The times we got out of school
  To watch his high school plays
We loved when he sung "Mammy"
  Those were fun-filled days…

So sad that circumstances
  Drifted us all apart
"Thank God, we had a second chance
  To rejuvenate our heart"…

For now its just farewell
  His life has just begun
He's there with his Carol
  His parents, "dad" my son…

They really haven't left us Missy
  Heaven is for eternity
Some glorious day again,
  We will all be a family…

And This Is What He Promised Us— Even Eternal Life... 1 John 3-25

I said a special prayer for you
   to take your pain away
On this your worst tragedy
   you must face today

Now you must say farewell
   to the man you dearly love
Asking God to shower you
   with strength from above

He was Albert William Davis
   to the first two people who loved him
To 3 sissy's and younger brother
   all held a love deep within

To Wanda, he was her soul mate
   her husband for 55 years
Her protector—supporter—friend
   her love, unconditionally sincere

To Marsha, Mary Beth and Butch
   he was daddy—Father or DAD
I've asked our "Heavenly Father"
   to comfort your hearts — so sad

To his Grand and Great-Grand children
   he was Cramps or grandpa
Wearing his heart on his sleeve for them
   in their eyes, he was 10 feet tall

To Jean—Clara—Marylou and Sonny
   he was the GREATEST of bros.
Always there if they needed him—
   a brother who couldn't say no

To many of you he was a friend
   one you'll miss very much
Always eager to lend a hand
   to add his magical touch

He was a very caring uncle
   this he showed to me
As to many nieces and nephews
   and to his cousins was he

Uncle Bud is sure handsome—I'd think
   and Aunt Wanda sure has the looks
It was very obvious—
   this man she had hooked

He always showed his love to us
   playing horsey on his knee
Or Patty-cake—singing songs
   or saying our ABC's

I remember like it was yesterday
   Uncle Bud said to me—
Do I call you Sissy or Yvonne—
   now that you're 23

I had been married and divorced
  with 3 little ones
But I was still his Sissy
  he said just having fun

Bud was a soft spoken man
  with kids he loved to tease
A man of few words
  a man who loved to please

Bud had a heart of GOLD
  and it was broken by his son
BUT HE WAS STILL HIS SON——
  no matter what he had done

It took time to forgive him
  of course their love did mend
We had "CHURCH" together said Butch
  he loved his dad—his friend

I prayed I could show him—
  I had truly changed my ways
I prayed I'd get that chance
  before this tragic day

Butch didn't get his wish
  but he knows it's not good-bye
He will see his dad again—
  in the mansion in the sky

To God—Bud was His son
  as Butch was to his dad
As our Father in Heaven forgives us
  Bud had to forgive his lad

God took Bud "HOME" quickly
  to HEAVEN—have NO DOUBT
He suffers NO more PAIN
  HALLELUJAH—we must SHOUT!!!!

I had asked God for a sign
  to show me he was there
A picture of Bud, Wanda, Jean and mom
  appeared out of no where

It was in the middle of my miniature angels
  which made no sense at all
It was taken 9 years and 50 pounds ago
  my memory recalls

It was truly mystifying
  as I cried a prayer again.
"Let me know somehow Lord
  that salvation was given to him"

I prayed that same prayer
  in church that very night
Asking for strength for Wanda—
  to keep His arms around them tight

I got the sad news that evening
  that it was 4:45 about
When Gods' angel took him "HOME"
  as I painfully did shout

It really didn't occur to me
  until the next day
I had found that picture
  "about" the time he passed away

God WAS giving me my sign
   I just didn't see
Bud was surrounded by HIS ANGELS
   God was telling me

What an awesome God we serve
   that He loves us all so much
To give us peace of mind
   with a gentle—loving touch

He loved His son, Albert enough
   to take him home quick
'No more pain He said—
   in HEAVEN I will fix'

His body is now healthy
   running streets of gold
Hugging his mom and dad
   in a land so beautiful, I'm told

He'll be missed daily
   but great memories we will cherish
God always gives us strength—
   when our love-ones perish

We will not say GOOD-BYE
   for you CAN see him again—
If you accept Christ as your Saviour
   ask forgiveness for your sins...

When God sends sorrow
  or some dreaded affliction
Be assured that it comes
  with His kind benediction.

By — Helen Steiner Rice

I will turn their mourning into
  joy... I will comfort them, and
give them gladness for sorrows...
    Jerimiah 31-13

Free of Pain – Alas

Today we are all sadden
   for our love one has passed
Yet we should rejoice
   for he is free of pain—alas

When Bill was a youngster
   polio seeked him out
In deep agony—
   this suffering child would shout

For years he fought this daily
   he knew no peace from pain
Would he ever walk again??
   or be forever lame?!

Now once again he suffered
   for the past couple of years
Other illnesses attacked
   and bought back his fears

Oh no said Bill—
   I won't go through this again
No more operations!
   he told family and friends

He had suffered most of his life
   ENOUGH!!—he finally said
I think that his decision
   by Christ was strongly led

I believe God lets us know
   when it is our time
To shed this earthly body
   so peace we will find

Bill was a giving man
   this was easy to see
When you looked into his eyes—
   they sparkled so happily

His smile was sincere and warm
   as also was heart
We will miss him deeply
   his memory will never part

He was a wonderful father
   his whole life through
And to all of his grandchildren
   a great grandpa too

Bill also loved Lous' kids
   as they also did him
He became their father
   when theirs was taken from them

He wasn't just a husband to Lou
   they were very best of friends
Giving to each other daily
   their love from deep within

Their love came at a time
   they needed it most
To help each other daily
   with life to cope

131

Although it was a short time
   he came into the Davis's lives
We thank our heavenly Father
   he chose Mary Lou for his wife

We thank God for sharing—
   this man with us all
We pray now for strength
   in this need, we call

Someday, we'll meet again
   as we will all of our loves
Now he is free of pain—
   in the arms of God above—

Becky

Becky was in her early fifties when she lost her long-time battle to multiple sclerosis. She had been ill for most of her adult life, as had been her husband, Donny who preceded her in death.

My sister, Donna, and I were the same ages as Becky and her sister Roberta. We loved to go to their house to play. Becky was a beautiful little girl and was always healthy as a child. I felt so sorry for her as I often thought of how cute and full of life she had been during her childhood and now she could hardly walk. Eventually, she was confined to a wheelchair and lived on oxygen and had to have in-home care.

Aunt Jean, her mom, was such a blessing to her daughter. I thank God my aunt is a Christian and I know she went to Him for strength through Becky's entire illness and especially at the time of her death.

I know how hard it is to watch your child suffer, and from my own son's death. I see it as a mixed feeling of rejoicing and loss, when they go home to be with the Lord. Our greatest hope, because of the love of Jesus, is joining them in Paradise for eternity.

I know Aunt Jean misses Becky, but she is looking forward to seeing her body made whole, as my Raymond's. We see them running together on God's land as they haven't done here on earth for many years. Until that glorious day comes, we will give God the glory for taking away their suffering.

The Heart of God is Mercy

To give ones life for another
   is the deepest love one can give
That's what Jesus did for us
   so eternal life we'd live

To sacrifice His Son to die
   is what God did out of love
No greater love has been given
   than our Father's from above

No one knows better than God
   what pain is all about
He too watched in agony
   as He heard his Son shout

That's how He knows, Aunt Jean
   the pain that's in your heart
But you'll see her again in heaven
   there, you'll never have to part

He understood Becky's pain
   said, "Daughter, time to come home
There's no suffering here
   and it's a beautiful place to roam."

I know there is no greater pain
   than your child, who precedes you in death
Your heart felt like it's breaking
   as they take that final breath

The Holy Spirit will give you strength
  He still gives it to me
Whenever I think of Raymond
  He comforts so tenderly

I say, "Thank you dear God,
  my Ray, suffers no more
Someday, he will greet me
  at Your heaven's door."

The loss of Becky will be great
  as the days go by
You will miss her greatly
  and ask God Why?!!

I will pray for you and your loved ones
  to help you through the day
Keep your eyes on the Lord
  You'll have peace when you pray.

Remember Me With Love

Oh what a glorious day—
As we have gathered here
We have come to say farewell
To one we love so dear

We are not saying goodbye
For we will see him again
He well welcome us "home"
All his family and friends

Jim lived a Christian life
In every way he could
Sharing the love of God
Just like Jesus would

He chose the nursing field
To heal bodies as well as souls
Just as Jesus did
The greatest physician we know

And oh how he loved children
He taught them the years through
At Kings Academy
As Jesus our King did too!

Jim and Esther could not have children
They said "this just won't do"
So God blessed them with Rebecca and Michael
To give their love to

He blessed them once again
With another bundle of joy
Rebecca had their first grandchild
A beautiful baby boy

This child he loved deeply
And showed it in many ways
"He's the twinkle in my eyes"
Jordan's grandpa would proudly say

He made sure Jordan knew Jesus
Sending him to Christian school
Taking him to church and Awana's
And teaching him God's golden rules

He got peace when Jordan got baptized
Just as God knew he would be
Which is why God allowed it
Before Jim went to eternity

Mike and Tracy gave them a grandson too
Little "M" he's affectionately called
He will have to hear the stories
Of his wonderful grandpa

Raise him as your dad would Mike
He wants him to know
That Jesus really loves him
The Bible tells him so

There is nothing Jim wanted more
Than for his kids and grandkids too
To live their life for Christ
To do what Jesus would do

We don't get to heaven
Riding on a loved ones shirt tail
Know Jesus as your Lord and Savior
Or no Heaven on your death trail

Jim's brothers and sisters at Forest Hill Alliance
Will miss this godly man
Always there for everyone
Giving a helping hand

He was on the Board of Evangelism
An Elder for many years
A leader in the Awana's
He loved them all so dear

Jim definitely was a veteran
He served in two, not one
In the Army and in the Air Force
I guess the Navy and Marines were no fun

He volunteered at JFK Hospital
For numerous years
Just because he loved people
And wanted to give them cheer

Jim lived for 72 years
Now it was his time to rest
God said "come home son
So you I can bless."

You have been a faithful servant
My will you have done
You have won many souls, Jim
"Thank you", my good son

God gave time for Jim's loved ones
To say farewell and let go
He also gave them peace
Before he left this earth below

I believe God sent two angels
To show Jim "home" that day
Jim kept repeating — "Hattie and Reinhold"
Esther's parents names he'd say

Even in our darkest hour
God sends us His brightest light
That his son, Jesus
He shines the way for our flight

Jim will be missed greatly
But I, as well as you
Can count ourselves blessed
For knowing him years through

Rebecca and Mike remember
What a special dad he was to you
How he treasured his children
Now live your life for him too

Jordan, you were very blessed
You had 10 great years
With a grandpa who loved you
So deep, so sincere

Just remember loved ones
He's not so far away
Close your eyes, feel your heart
That's where he will stay

He will be there for you
As he was on this land
Just ask God for a special angel
To send this caring man

Jim was a very happy man
He certainly lived a full life
He was married for 45 years
To a loving and caring wife

No doubt Esther will miss him
But she knows in her heart
The memories that they shared
Never will they part

She will see her Jim again
He'll greet her at the pearly gates
Welcome home my darling wife
Now eternity awaits

I will show you our mansion
First meet our wonderful master
Then we will walk on streets of gold
We'll talk and share lots of laughter

Remember how I use to dream
Of traveling all over the place
Now I go wherever I will
Flying at angels pace

How Do You Say Good-Bye

How do you say goodbye
  to someone that you love
First you pray for strength
  from Our Lord above

You close your eyes and reminisce
  of all the yesteryears
You thank God for this time
  to share with your sweet dear

Time to thank your love one
  for all he's done for you
Tell him what a Blessing he's been
  all the years through

Wrap your arms around him
  give a big hug and kiss
Softly whisper in his ear
  he'll be deeply missed

Now it's time to "LET GO AND LET GOD"
  send his Angels down here
Doug will be set free of pain
  so please have no fear

He'll be in the arms of Jesus
  his body will be made new
He'll prepare a mansion
  while he waits for you

God with his sense of humor
  might give Doug a mansion to "FIX"
After all he is "Mr. Fix It"
  and boy will Doug love this

I'm sure he'll need some "DUCK TAPE"
  so we would recognize his place
What! NO DUCK TAPE?!
  THIS PLACE IS A DISGRACE!!

Course there will be a FISHING POND
  the best you've ever seen
Just waiting for Grandson Brian
  to share in this Beautiful 'Dream'

A special swing he'll put on the porch
  to hold Kristin on his lap
She's Rougher then a cob, he'll say
  his grand-daughter sure loved her Pap

For his sweet grand-daughter Sarah
  he loves with all his heart
He'll have a place for Sadie Joan
  from this cat he cannot part!

I'm sure there'll be some job
  he'll need an extra hand
He'll wait for the son he loves
  when he leaves the earthly land

Until that time comes Doug
  I think it would be GREAT
Each year on your Birthday
  your Dad's re-birth celebration

And for his "little girl" April
  will keep her in your care
As will all his Grandchildren
  and Pam too will be there

I'm sure my sister Pam
  Doug will give our love to Dad
Dad will warmly welcome him
  which makes our hearts all glad

And as for his beloved Peggy
  his soul-mate for 49+ years
He'll ask God for Amazing Grace
  to shed on his loving dear

Just hold onto the memories Peg
  when your hearts become as one
Sharing laughs and tears
  from morning 'til night is done

Now close your eyes everyone
  see Doug is smiling again
No more pain-his body made new
  his life did just begin

Doug will have Eternal Joy
  and you can have it too
Know Jesus as your Lord Savior
  the Kingdom will be given to you

HOW DO YOU SAY GOOD-BYE
  you don't my dear friends
You say FAREWELL my sweet man
  'til we see you again

Thank God for the Time You Had

Often I feel very sad
  when I think of my beloved son
I think about the yesteryears
  laughing and having fun

When, that pain gets really bad
  and I long to hold my Ray
I think of the things he did
  before he went away

Like the time a can hit him
  when he went out to play
That accident could've been fatal
  he was only five that day

He was also just five
  when he scared me to death
He pulled over a refrigerator
  I could only hold my breath!

His body layed beneath it
  but he was O.K.
One again — Once again
  God saved him that day

Or the time he was playing
  and fell through a grass door
He was cut from head to toe
  but he was only sore

Again it could've been fatal
   this time he was just seven
I thank our merciful God
   as I cried out to the heavens

The list goes on and on
   of Raymond's accidents
So I thank my loving God
   for the years together we spent

I had 31 years
   to love my little boy
It could've been far less
   but God game me that joy

Instead of feeling bitter
   I thank the Lord above
For giving me those extra years
   to share with my love

As a Christian, I also know
   someday I'll see my Ray
When God beckons me home
   OH! What a great day!

I know you're feeling pain Andy
   but thank God for what you had
A relationship kids desire
   with a friend you called 'dad'

God is a caring Father
   and you are His child too
He'll help you if you ask Andy
   give strength to pull you through

Devon will also miss him
   she too loved that man
She will be there for you
   reach out and take her hand

You will have those days Andy
   you will miss him extra much
Close your eyes and reminisce
   you'll feel his gentle touch...

Love One Another

"To My Dear Friend," "Sammy,"
   this is "Especially For You
Just to let you know You are Tops"
   and to say, "God Bless You."

"Walking By Faith," Sam,
   you said, "He leadeth Me,"
To give "Joy To The World,"
   to "The Most Precious Gift Of Them All" — Family!

"God's Love Is Reflected In You"
   through your "Precious Moments," Sam
By sharing "High Hopes" —
   "You've Touched So Many Hearts," in this land

You are "Serving The Lord"
   spreading "Brotherly Love"
You, "Let the Whole World Know"
   through your talent, "Sent From Above"

You are, "Making A Joyful Noise"
   as you "Prepare The Day Of The Lord," Sam,
"What A Difference You've Made In My Life," and others
   so, "Press On," — keep ministering, my man!

You are a "Shepherd of Love"
   for you know, "What The World Needs Is Love"
"Sowing The Seeds Of Kindness"
   showing, "Happiness Is The Lord" — above

"For God So Loved The World,"
  "God Cared Enough To Send His Best"
"The Sweetest Name I Know"
  "His Name Is Jesus," came to BLESS!!

"God Sent You Just In Time"
  "To Let The Whole World Know"
"The Good Lord Always Delivers"
  "God's Promises Are Sure," — and that is SO!

"To Tell The Truth You're Special"
  you, "Brighten Someone's Day"
"Making Spirits Bright" —
  saying, "Jesus Is The Only Way"!!

"We Need A Good Friend Through The Rough Times,"
  so, "Take It To The Lord In Prayers"
"There's A Light At The End Of The Tunnel"
  "The Sun Is Always Shinning Somewhere"

When "Philip" went to be "Safe In The Arms Of Jesus,"
  you knew, "The Lord Will Carry You Through" —
You had to "Trust In The Lord" —
  for "He's The Healer Of Broken Hearts," too

"But Love Goes On Forever" —
  "Time Heals" and "This Too Shall Pass'
For years you are "Growing In Grace"
  "Prayer Changes Things" so fast!

One day you'll be "Going Home" —
  singing, "Happy Days Are Here Again"!!
"This Is Your Day To Shine," saith the Lord —
  for giving "Precious Moments" to the end —

"Philip," went to be "Standing In The Presence Of
    The Lord,"
  waiting "Especially For Eve"
"Isn't He Precious," he says to the Lord —
    Daddy, "Thee I Love," — "I Still DO"!!

You will "Enter His Court With Thanksgiving"
    for there's "No Tears Past The Gate"
You come to "Hallelujah Square" —
    where "Ray" and "Guardian Angels" await!!

"You're Worth Your Weight In Gold," "Sammy"
    always, "You Serve With A Smile" —
"You Can Fly," home someday —
    but "Sammy," not in a long while!!

"My (our) Days Are Blue Without You"
    "To Some Bunny Special," we say
"Who's Gonna FILL Your Shoes?" "Sammy"
    COLOR OUR WORLD BLUE LIKE THE ANGEL —
        that day!!

"You Will Always Be Our Hero" —
    for teaching "It's Better To Give Than To Receive"
We are "Friends To The Very End" —
    for "Friendship Grows When You Plant A Seed"!!

"His Love Will Shine On You," Sam
    for "Sharing Begins In The Heart"
I'm (we) "So Glad You Fluttered Into My (our) Life"
    for "Friends Never Drift Apart"

"I (we) Belong To The Lord"
   for "We Are ALL Precious In His Sight"
We are "Thanking Him For You"
   "Sending You Oceans Of Love Tonight"

"This Day Has Been Made In Heaven"
   for "We Have Come From Afar"
We give you "A Bouquet From God's Garden Of Love"
   because a "Prince Of A Guy You Are"!!

"We Are God's Workmanship" —
   thus, "To God Be The Glory"
"Blessed Are The Peacemakers"
   "Love One Another," is God's Story!!

"I (we) Get A Kick Out Of You," "Sammy,"
   as you "Smile Along The Way"
And you sing, "He Is MY Song"
   and "He Walks With Me," all day!!

"The Eyes Of The Lord Are Upon You,"
   as you march "Onward Christian Soldiers"
Teaching, "Love Is Sharing"
   and to "Trust And Obey" is kosher!!

If there are "Angels On Earth" —
   "You Deserve A Halo — Thank You"
For you are an "Angel Of Mercy" —
   and "You Deserve An Ovation" too!!

"May God Bless You With Rainbows," "Sammy"
   "May Your Every Wish Come True"
We say, "Cheers To The Leader"
   and may God "Bless-Um You"!!!!

Anthony

Anthony was a mentally challenged young man, in his forties, who lived at home with his mother. Every day he would wait for his Mama on the porch to come home from work. Anthony was a loving, giving, young man, who loved his Mama very much, as she did him.

I heard about Anthony from my long-time friend, Jo Bowling. We worked in Isgro's Restaurant about thirty-three years ago and have remained in touch. Anthony's mother use to come to the Italian eatery, as she was a friend of the owners. Jo thought I'd remember her, but I didn't. Jo didn't call me too often so I knew his death touched her deeply, as she kept repeating how much the mother would miss him and how hard it would be living there without him waiting on the porch for her every day.

As soon as we hung up, the Lord gave me the poem for Anthony's Mama. I felt as though Anthony was telling me every word! I wrote this poem in about 10-15 minutes, then I called Jo back and read it to her. She was quiet for a minute (which is a miracle in itself for this Italian lady) then said, "Yvonne, you wrote that poem that quick—we just hung up!" I said, "Yes—but I didn't do it alone, as God is the one who tells me what to write!" In this case, I think God allowed Anthony to tell me what he wanted to say to his Mama.

She really loved it and asked me if I would send her a copy. I sent one to her and of course for "Mama." Jo told me later how much she loved it and it did help Mama through the loss of her Anthony. She has since moved to Florida and said she reads the poem every day where it hangs framed on her wall. It gave her peace of mind to know that he is with the Lord, knowing she will be there one day too.

Hello Mama!

I'm in Heaven with God —
  oh, what a wonderful place!!
I'm here with my friend, Jesus,
  He has such a beautiful face!!

I'm sorry I had to leave you —
  but we'll be together again,
That's what Jesus told me
  when your new life begins

The only key to His Kingdom —
  is to believe in Jesus Christ
Believe He is your Saviour —
  He died to give us "Life"

"Eternal Life," in Heaven Mama!!!
  oh, this place is great!!!
I can't wait to see you again —
  we'll meet at the Pearly Gate!!

You know, I'm not sick anymore
  my body, Jesus made new!!
And when you meet Jesus —
  He'll heal your body too!!

I'm getting our new "home" ready
  it's a big mansion, you know —
I'll be waiting on the porch for you
  like I did on earth below —

I had to let you know, Mama —
   that I am really O.K.
I know how much you miss me —
   more and more each day —

Please be happy for me, Mama —
   no longer am I in pain —
I'm walking streets of GOLD!!
   where Jesus Christ reigns

I haven't left you completely —
   close your eyes and see —
Feel your heart beating —
   that's your little Anthony ...

Love you — see you in the Kingdom!!

Barry Grunow

Barry Grunow had been a great son, a loving father, a caring husband, a friend to many, a respected teacher, a role model to numerous kids and most importantly, a child of God. Unfortunately, at the hand of one of his students, he was shot down in his early thirties. The question why has yet to be answered. Even the young thirteen year old, Nathaniel, had no answer. In fact, he said Mr. Grunow was his favorite teacher as he was to most of his students at the Lake Worth Middle School. He really didn't know why he shot him, he just did. How sad is that?

Nathaniel is to be tried as an adult, so if found guilty, his life too will end. My heart goes out to the Grunow Family, as well as to the loved ones of Nathaniel. Because no matter what he did, he is still their child and they love him as much as ever. This is how our Heavenly Father is. No matter what terrible sin we have committed, He has already forgiven us. We don't know the outcome for Nathaniel, but as for Mr. Grunow, I believe he is in the arms of his Lord.

I didn't know Mr. Grunow personally, but I did attend one of his numerous funeral services, which was televised all over the U.S. It brought back the sad memories of Columbine. The tears that were shed by his co-workers, students, loved ones and numerous people, who never met him, showed how much this man loved and would be missed. Much has been done for his family in his memory, but we know nothing can be done to take away that stabbing pain we all feel when our child leaves too soon.

This terrible tragedy was just a reminder of the senseless kids killing kids, their teachers and too often, even their parents for stupid reasons or just for the hell of it.

Speaking of hell, I truly believe what I said in the poem...when God got kicked out of the schools, Satan came slithering in. The lack of morality is evident in our children today. They show no respect for their teachers, parents, peers, the law themselves and especially God's laws. Satan's influence is seen and heard in their dress, words, actions, music, video games, board games, dancing, drugs and their attitude in general. The word God is only used in vain and in hatred mockery. Kids who commit horrific crimes, often admit they heard voices telling them to kill, as in the case of the Columbine killers. Satanic type videos and a movie was their influence.

There have been too many of these sad headlines in the past ten years. It is time to put God back in our schoolhouses, our homes and the White House.

When adults start admitting that this is the problem, we need to kick Satan out and get on our knees and ask God for direction, our kids will be saved. There has already been too many good teachers such as Barry and too much innocent blood shed.

Wake up America—before your child is taken at the hand of Satan's slayers!

Remember Me With Love

Why did this have to happen?
  to one who cared so much
His goal in life was evident
  young lives he had to touch

This Barry Grunow did daily
  but not just in school
At home, the game field, wherever ...
  he taught Life's Golden Rules

The rule of love, Mr. G. taught
  by the way, he lived his life
The best daddy to Sam and Lee-Ann
  a great husband to Pamela, his wife

We all have been cheated
  those who knew him well — and Not
One thing is for certain
  he will never be forgot

The halls of Lake Worth Middle
  will be haunting this coming year
The love and laughter of Mr. Grunow
  will be deafening to our ears

Don't let his death be in vain
  something must be done
Before the hand of death
  takes away your loved one

What is the solution?
  it's happening more every day
No — it's not JUST the GUNS
  taking our loved ones away

Some kids lack their own identity
  they are like hollow shells
They have no respect for life
  they live in their own world of hell

What's wrong with our children
  are we reaping what we've sown
Killing our un-born and aging
  is this the message we've shown?

When did this all begin?
  Killing teachers and kids in school
THOU SHALT NOT KILL — NOT A SUGGESTION
  it's God's Golden Rule!!

God? Oh, yes, remember Him?
  one whose name we forget to call
Unless we shout it in vain
  or a crisis on us befalls

Honor thy Father and thy Mother
  God commands us of this
Can we blame JUST our kids
  when parents lack to hug and kiss

Do we show our Affection?
  Are we Available to them?
Do they know our Appreciation?
  and real Acceptation from within

Are we Zealous about their activities?
  Or do we know Zip what they do?
Have they become walking Zombies?
  life meaning Zero each day through

How well do you know your children?
  write between my A's and Z's
Do you say, "I love you?"
  "How proud you are and pleased?"

When God got kicked out of school
  Satan came slithering in
Morals became a foreign word
  killing the answer — not a sin

Will your child be the next one?
  to pull the trigger on the gun?
Oh, no he is an honor student
  in sports he is number one

So was Nathaniel Brazill
  he was a likable, funning kid
Good grades in school —
  in music was a Whiz

When you start to miss me
  close your eyes my dear
Listen to your heart beat
  that's where I'll be near

Take care of mom, my brother
  she really needs you now
Pray to God for strength
  He'll get you through somehow

Today we all MOURN DEATH
   it has cheated not one but two
If Mr. G. was here —
   I think he'd say this to you

Satan is controlling our kids
   that's why all the killings
Through Videos, Porno and Drugs
   they find this all so thrilling

"Remember with love," he'd say
   "do WHAT JESUS WOULD DO
To forgive is Godly, he'd say
   that's what I want of you"

I'm so sorry I had to leave
   without saying goodbye
But hush, all my loved ones
   for me please don't cry

I am in a wonderful place
   There is no violence here
Mom, Dad meet me at Heaven's Gate
   so I have no fear

Take care of my babies, Pam
   I'll be watching over you
I'll be your special angel
   in the day and night too

To parents, family, and friends
   don't let my death be in vain
Make this problem go away —
   from Satan take the reins

Put God back in your homes
  put God back in your schools
Put God back in America
  or Satan continues to RULE!

A Mother's Worst Fear

I know your heart is breaking
  as I know how you feel
I lost my son, Raymond
  because he was ill

I'm sure it is different
  when he is suddenly taken away
I waited dreadfully —
  for the hand of death, each day

No matter how they die
  that stabbing pain is there
There is nothing in life
  which we can compare

Although he was a man —
  he was still your little boy,
He was such a good son —
  giving you so much joy

How proud Barry made you
  through his thirty-five years
It seems like only yesterday
  you held your baby near

He made you a happy Grandma
  having Sam and Lee-Anne
Of course he had some help —
  from his beautiful wife, Pam

How ironic on this day —
  we say farewell to your son
Today I will welcome —
  the birth of my grandson

I know they will all miss him
  but I know you will be there
To tell them of daddy's love
  how much he deeply cared

His "other kids" will miss him
  his students he so loved
I'm sure he'll be watching them
  from his classroom up above

You will have your "Barry Days"
  the days you miss him Extra much
Close your eyes, think of him —
  and all the lives he touched

You will feel his warmth —
  see his smiling face
Know that he is well —
  in God's loving embrace

He will be with his dad
  as they both prepare
The beautiful mansion
  when you're welcome home there

It is not goodbye you say
  it is only farewell
You will see your son again —
  this, I honestly tell

I pray that all the hatred —
  in this world goes away
Until that day comes —
  for all our children, I pray ...

Brian

Brian was a young man, in his mid-twenties, married and had one little boy. Brian was graduating from med-school and had told his wife, he had always wanted to climb a mountain in N. Carolina, where they were at the time. He went with a team of climbers as he was definitely an amateur in this field, and felt safer with them. It was winter time but the weather had been great with no snow predicted. Without any warning, a quick change brought a heavy snow fall and freezing weather, which killed all of the climbers before rescuers could reach them.

When the parents of Brian told the story of Brian's death, in our Bible class, there wasn't a dry eye. The excitement of their son becoming a doctor was soon overshadowed by his unexpected death. I had known of the parents for numerous years from the local neighborhood lounge, where we all gathered before becoming Christians. We were all friends with the owner, who later in the next year, lost his stepchild, Rusty, which I have written about in this book.

This is the couple who gave a poem, by an unknown artist, to Rusty's parents. They wanted to tell them how God had been their strength through their loss, as He would be for them. It was this poem, which I spilled coffee on, and as I wiped it off with a napkin, a rose appeared! Not just any rose—it looked just like the one my son, Raymond, always drew for me!

Brian's Song... I Choose to Follow You

Most are not as blessed —
   the way you were, my friends
To have had a son, — a brother — a friend
   who was the greatest to the end

His love for life was evident
   as was his love for people too
He lived life to its fullest —
   his motto, "What Would Jesus Do!"

The love for his family was evident
   like things he did for you —
When it came to Nicole and Kayla
   his love always shined through

His faithful dog was a Rottweiller,
   who was given to him as a gift
He went with Brian everywhere
   his spirits, Norman would lift

Brian's first love was for the Lord
   singing songs to Him in praise
With the voice of an angel —
   he'd melt your heart away

Now his voice is silent
   to his loved ones on earth
He's singing in the choir of angels
   since he began his rebirth

As Christians we all know
   Brian again you'll see
He will welcome you all home
   for life eternity

Brian's time here on earth —
   was very short in years
But he lived every day —
   with enthusiasm sincere

He enjoyed many sports —
   FISHING and softball, #1
Sometimes bowling and golfing
   the also played for fun

Brian loved all music
   his favorite Christian and Country, of course
He loved dressing like a cowboy —
   all he needed was a horse!

As much as Brian loved people —
   they in return loved him
This was shown in multitude
   when Brian's life would end

South Palm Community
   where Brian worshipped the Lord
Were there to comfort the family
   in honor of the man they adored

Pastor Coleman preached so great on
   "Four Things" Brian would want you to know
Even after Brian's death —
   his love still touched souls

Those he had invited to church —
   but never did attend
Until they honored this wonderful man
   they proudly called their friend

God took this terrible tragedy
   and turned it into good
"Brian wasn't just a great fisherman," said Angie
   "He was a 'fisher of men,' in the hood"...

The City of Lake Worth
   where Brian worked each day
Poured out their love —
   in numerous ways

They sent beautiful flowers
   and gave a collective gift
A burial spot near his home
   giving all hearts a lift

They also flew the flag, half-mast
   not one day, but all week
And as a lasting memory —
   gave Brian his own Street...

All total, twenty-four people
   directly will be saved
These lives can touch others
   in the same loving way

Each time you ache to see Brian
   peacefully close your eyes
Vision him catching humongous fish as
   he jumps with joy and surprise!!

His softball team also rallied —
  holding a special tribute too
Brian's No. 7, was retired —
  and a gift was presented to you

How appropriate this number —
  for God's number is also 7
I think he's wearing No. 7 now —
  playing softball in the heavens

The list of friends are numerous —
  who helped in different ways —
Like Chuck who prepared Brian's music
  at the funeral it was played

Without this show of love —
  from Brian's family and friends
The pain could've been worse —
  so thank you from within

Brian is missed deeply —
  but his legacy of giving continues
By being an Organ Donor —
  lives have been made anew

Brian's love will keep on "BEATING"
  after death as in life —
His heart saved a woman from dying
  she was a mother and a wife ...

Thank God for sharing His child
  for Brian was God's son too
Then listen to Brian's Song —
  "I CHOOSE TO FOLLOW YOU" ...

Only God Knows Why

Why, God, Why?
  I shouted through tears
Why, God, Why?
  he lived so few years

This was my cry —
  as I held my child
I knew he'd be with God
  in just a short while

Each day I live this pain
  so I go to God in prayer
I know that His strength
  is ALWAYS there

He too knows that pain
  for He gave his only son
To suffer and die for us all
  our souls He had won

"But Your Son came back to Life!"
  I heard myself say
Yes, so yours could have eternal life
  from that very day!

Someday we will see our sons
  as they sit by God's side
They will welcome us all home
  with their arms open wide

We know not why —
   why God took them home to stay
They were his children first
   before born that special day

Although my heart still grieves
   I thank the Lord above
For sharing His child with me
   he gave us so much love

The memories I will treasure
   about my "little" boy
He gave me so many tears —
   much laughter and joy ...

Although he's not with me
   we really aren't apart
I feel his love within me
   with every beat of my heart

We know not why today ...
   why Brian had to go
But someday, God will reveal...
   this I personally know

Brian's love will continue
   through his child, God's given you
When you look into his eyes
   Brian's love will shine through

So when your heart is grieving
   just remember my friend
Your next meeting with Brian
   will never come to an end ...

David

I had known David for about two years from where we worked together in a restaurant called *Chef Mingo* (short for Flamingo, the Florida bird.) Shortly after he had started there, he said he was in need of a place to rent, so I rented him a room in my house. It was convenient for him as I was close to our work and I had a car, which he didn't.

Dave was a partier as I was too in those days, so I could handle his drinking. It became a little hard for me when I stopped drinking, so it caused a problem between us. I loved him like a brother, but was old enough to be his mom. We had many long talks, and after a few drinks, he poured his heart out to me. He told me he knew when he was very young he preferred boys to girls and how it caused problems with his family. He loved his mother very much and never wanted to hurt her. His mom and him kept in touch a lot at my house, so I knew there was no problem with them.

Dave had a companion named Tim, he had known for about eight years or more. Tim was a super nice guy. He was tall, good looking, intelligent and fun to be around. I welcomed Tim into my house, but David knew I didn't allow him to spend the night. How David lived his life was his business, but what went on in my house was mine. Most of the time, he respected that, but we did have a few quarrels about it.

I was glad David lived with me as I felt he needed a friend to talk to. He seemed so alone most of the time and unsure of himself. I had stopped drinking and partying as I said and found my way back to Christ. David would ask me questions about the Lord or the Bible usually when he was drinking, nonetheless, I would answer the questions he asked. I wanted him to know that he was loved by his heavenly Father, even though he never felt the love from his earthly father. I also wanted him to know God loved him so much, that He gave His own Son to die for him, so he could have the greatest happiness he would ever know. If only he believed in Jesus. I think my son's illness touched him and got him thinking about his own death and where he would end up. I thought maybe that was why I was put into David's life.

After Raymond's death, I decided to take a trip to Ohio to see my family, and David went to stay at Tim's mother's house for a while. Her being a Christian, did not allow the two to be romantically together in her house, so they had separate bedrooms.

I was gone for three weeks and when I came home Tim told me of the shocking news. David had died of an aneurysm. I was stunned speechless. It happened two days before I returned. I had missed the service for him but I did go to Tim's mother's house where they had held the memorial.

Tim told me Dave had moved out of his mother's home and was staying with a friend temporarily. Tim said, "He just felt it was better because his mother was having company and needed the space for them to stay there."

Throughout the conversation, I felt Tim was blaming himself for not being with him when it happened. "Dave had just gone in to his bed to go to sleep when it apparently happened," Tim said. "It was so quick, that his friend could do nothing except call the paramedics." "So what makes you think Tim, if you had been there, that you could've saved him?" I asked. "Usually when one has an aneurysm they go pretty quick. Even if someone is there with them there isn't much you can do, so I don't think it would've mattered." I knew he was feeling guilty, as I had said similar words when my son died.

Tim and David had known each other for about twelve years and had moved here from New York together, so I knew this was really hard on him and his family. I asked, "How Maxine (David's mother)was doing?" He said, "Not well at all." They had his body flown home at her request where they could have a service for his family and friends, as he had no family here. I told Tim and his family to call me if ever they needed to talk. Tim gave me a picture of David and I found some I gave to him.

I talked to Maxine sometime later as I wanted to give her time to get over the initial shock and the funeral. I don't remember if I called her or she me, but I do recall the sadness in her voice, as if it were hard for her to breathe, or talk at all. "He wanted to come to see me and I told him to wait a week or two or maybe even a month—I don't know why—I don't remember now," she seemed to be just rattling on. "He said he was having headaches—severe ones sometimes, do you think I should've been more concerned about his headaches?" she asked, still in a rambling manner. "If I had told him to come when he wanted to maybe he would still be alive."

Poor Maxine, I thought, she is having a mother's guilt, as I too had. Once again, I said to her what I had told Tim to try to ease the guilt and her pain. My heart went out to her as I felt her pain. I heard myself say all the whys, what ifs, the maybes, I should haves, etc., etc., just as this mother who was feeling helpless and lost.

It's been three years since David's death and Maxine and I are still in touch. She is sounding much stronger, but I know, like me, there are her good days and her "David Days." I pray for her as I do all those who are grieving over their child and I remind her that God is there for her. All she has to do is reach out to Him as He is waiting there to hear from her.

Only God Can Ease Your Pain

How do you mend a broken heart —
  of a mother who lost her son
A life taken suddenly
  before it hardly begun

I wish I knew the answer
  for I would gladly tell
I would put it in a bottle
  for all who face this hell

But there is no simple answer
  to take the pain away
The only peace I have found
  is to go to God and pray

I think about the good times
  we shared through the years
I thank God for sharing His child
  through eye-filled tears

Then I sobbed hysterically
  ask, "What should I have done
There must have been something — anything
  to have saved my son?"

Then I blamed myself
  for something stupid in the past
I know it wasn't my fault
  I quietly say — real fast

None of us, know our fate
   only our Lord, above
I pray he knew Christ as his Saviour
   and gave to Him his love

I also pray for you, Maxine
   for God to give peace to you
To set you free of any guilt
   for there was nothing you could do

But the guilt still lingers
   because I miss Raymond so
Oh, how I love him
   I need him to know!!

David knew how you felt, Maxine
   he loved you very much
He talked of you lovingly
   of your caring touch

You, like all mothers
   try to take the blame
Maybe from our past
   we feel guilt and shame

There was nothing we could do
   Their death was not caused
By me and not by you

David was like a son to me
   his death broke my heart
But I thank God for the time
   in his life, I had a part

We talked about the love of God
  and how He gave His Son to die
To save all of God's children
  eternal happiness — we're not denied

Please call me if you need me
  to talk or say a prayer
Or a shoulder to cry on
  I promise to be there

More importantly, Maxine
  God will help you through
Just go to Him and ask
  He is waiting there for you

Eric

My heart broke when I got the phone call from Kathy concerning Eric's death. Personally, I had never met him but I had known his family for over twenty years. My three older kids grew up with his mom, Nancy, and his three aunts, JoAnn, Sandy and Kathy.

Wayne the youngest of the siblings, played ball and grew up with my youngest son, Joe, which is how he met Eric. Joe didn't know Eric well, but was close to Wayne which was the reason Kathy was calling me

It wasn't the first time I had been called about their family tragedies and they had many through the years. In 1982, Kathy and her husband, Bruce, lost their daughter, Autum, shortly before she was one year old, of a disease. A few months later, once again tragedy knocked, with the news of the eldest sister, JoAnn, having cancer. Sandy, the third oldest donated her bone marrow, in hopes of saving her sister, but a few months later, the cancer won out, one week after her twenty-fourth birthday.

In 1989, once again the family was to get the bad news that their mother was now plagued with the same disease that took her eldest child. Within the year, Betty too had succumb to this terrible illness while still in her mid-forties.

But, it is so much easier when we have God there to carry us through the pain as He promised us in the Bible in Psalms 23:4, "Yea, though I walk through the valley of the shadow of death, I will fear no evil; for You are with me; Your rod and Your staff, they comfort me."

What is even better is just knowing Jesus as our Savior, means we will be in Heaven with Him one day, for eternal happiness as will all our loved ones who know Him—thus we will be with them again—forever! That's not a theory—

it's a fact! It is written in His word—the Bible! I am not anyone's judge—only God knows for sure who called on Him—even if it was in their last breathe.

I would like to say this is the end of the tragedies in this family but as of a few months ago, another blow has come to Randy and Sandy. Because of an injury at work, Randy went to the emergency room. After many tests, they realized that he was in serious trouble with his kidneys. He was told if they hadn't found his problem he would probably have died in about six months. He said he had no idea there was anything wrong with them. He had to start dialysis three times a week and he had to quit work immediately. He was put on the long waiting list for a life-saving kidney.

Once again life had dealt another bad hand to this family. With five kids to raise and an unknown future for this family, I pray they come to the Lord to help them through this long road of familiar pain.

Before Eric's death, Kathy and her family lost a dear friend who had been living with them for years, and was like a grandmother to them. She also died a quick, unexpected, death. Kathy phoned, asking me to write a poem for her funeral.

Now Eric who has just turned twenty-four, became the next victim of cancer. He was home on leave from the service and complained of his arm hurting, but was dismissed from doctors as probably an injury from ball or something. Returning to the service, after still having pain, the medics discovered the dreadful disease. Eric was sent back to the states to await his sentence. A short time later, once again their family was devastated as this too familiar villain snatched another of their loved ones.

Eric's death not only crushed his mother, Nancy, it deeply touched his Aunt Sandy and her husband, Randy, and all of their five kids, as they had been a big part of his young life. For personal reasons, Eric had lived with them for many years. They felt about him as they did their own kids. Eric as also very close to his grandpa, as they spent many hours fishing together, at their fishing camp.

I read Eric's poem at the funeral in hopes that it might touch the hearts of his family and young friends and bring them to knowing Jesus Christ as their Lord and Savior. My heart broke as I looked out at the room that night. This family had seen a lot of death for being so young, I thought. How in the world can they get through this without the help of God! None of them were Christians—none of them knew the Lord. Not that Christians don't face death or pain—trust me, I've had my share!

Eric's Farewell Love Letter

I heard you say, "I love you" —
   and it was alright to go
That meant so much to me
   I want you all to know

Then I heard God say —
   "Reach out, take my hand, —
It's time to come home, son —
   to your Promised Land ..."

I didn't want to leave you, Mom —
   I knew your heart would break
But my pain was so severe —
   no longer could I wait...

Angels came to take me home
   to my Heavenly Dad
He put His arms around me —
   Said, "Welcome HOME, my Lad"

Oh, what a wonderful Father!
   He's so good to me,
He made my body new
   of pain I'm set free!

This place is so awesome —
   I'm walking streets of gold!
I'm with Grandma Betty/Aunt Joann
   and there's others that I know

And Autum, she's so beautiful —
  Bruce and Kathy, she sends her love
And to little sis, Tonya —
  she's watching you from above

I thank you, Sandy and Randy
  for keeping me in your care —
Whenever I needed you —
  you were always there —

You treated me like your own son
  your whole family was great
Please live your life for Jesus
  so I can meet you at Heaven's Gate

I love you Shawna and Steven
  and Wayne, you were like my bro
God's Angels will surround you
  to protect you from life's foes

Catch a big one for me PaPa —
  and if you're feeling blue —
Think about the good times
  That I spent with you

And to my dear Mom —
  please take care of yourself
When your heart feels pain —
  only God can help ...

I told my Heavenly Father —
  I was worried about all of you
Because of the pain —
  I knew you were going through

He said He understood —
  for He felt that pain too —
When He watched His Son die slowly —
  out of love for me and you

It's too bad it takes Cancer
  or some other terrible thing
To find the love of Jesus
  and the peace only He can bring

God will help you through —
  if you go to Him in prayer
Nothing else will ease your pain
  I know I was there ...

Love,
Eric

The only "key" to Eternal Life, in seeing your loved ones again, is to know and accept Jesus Christ as your Lord and Saviour ...

Don't let Eric's death be in vain ...

John F. Kennedy, Jr.

There is nothing I can say about JFK, Jr., that hasn't been said throughout his short lived thirty-eight years. He was truly America's son from the day of his birth, November 25, 1960 to his shocking death, July 16, 1999. The Prince of Camelot was dead. America's "adopted" son, vanished into a temporary watery grave, along with his beautiful Princess and sister-in-law.

I, like millions in the world, cried as we had done on November 22, 1963 when John's father, our U.S. President, was so cruelly taken from us. He too, in the prime of life and the height of his career. John had such a future ahead of him and all America was anxious to know what it would be. Now, that answer will never be known.

To us mere mortals, I believe, we too often put famous people into a separate category than ourselves. John, like Elvis, John Lennon, Princess Diana, Marilyn Monroe, etc. are put on a pedestal and although we admire them from afar, we feel we know them almost as well as a member of our own family. Their early demise from this world not only shocks us, it brings us to realize they are only human, just as we are. They are just as capable of dying at anytime—any age, just as we.

I was truly upset over John-John's death as I was over his father's death thirty-seven years before. Although we lost a beautiful person, the really sad fact is we lost three beautiful people.

The Bassette Family who lost their two daughters were put into the shadow of John's death. Their pain was as real as was the Kennedy's, if not twice as much. My heart truly went out to them as I know the pain of a death of a child, thank God, not two—and at the same time. They too were young, with I'm sure bright futures ahead of them, when they unexpectedly died. Their parents loved them as we loved our kids when they were taken too quickly.

As the light of the Kennedy Family and the lights of the Besette Family dimmed into darkness. I prayed to the God of Light and Eternal Life to give peace to these two families.

American's Favorite Son

A silence filled the land
  around the world the day
Another terrible tragedy
  came the Kennedy's way

It was to be a joyous occasion
  but it wasn't going to be
American's favorite son —
  was swallowed by the sea

We were all in disbelief
  when the news crossed our screens
It brought back memories
  of his father's deadly scene

Prayers of hope were lifted
  please he wouldn't die
It would take a miracle
  from this crash to survive

My first thought was of his mother
  thank God she's not here
To face the greatest of pain
  to lose her son, John dear

Then I thought of Caroline
  oh no! I thought, so sad
She has lost her whole family
  her mother, brother and dad

I know she won't be alone
   for the Kennedys are a close family
They will be there to comfort her
   but she'll long for he

We grieved when his father died
   and our hearts would break too
When John-John saluted the casket
   impacting a memory, years through

Like any parent, we cheered —
   when John passed the bar
I think he did it for his mother
   it was the least of his forte, by far

His heart wasn't in it
   this was obvious to see
He chose to write and publish
   this was the field for he

His creativeness in "George"
   would make his mom and dad proud
When it came to politics
   he boasted his opinion loud

Aunt Rosemary and Kathleen
   Uncle Joe and Bobby too
There's David and Michael —
   the whole Kennedy crew!!!

We know not why, —
   this tragedy came to be
But it is so ironic
   he died in the sea—

John wasn't just her brother
  he was also her good friend
Always there for each other
  through many tragic ends

Although she was the oldest
  it was John she looked up to
He was the glue, that bonded them
  when tragedy they went through

John was very successful —
  he reached it not by fame
It was hard work and determination
  not the Kennedy name

That's why he was loved
  in all America's hearts
Not just his good looks —
  but in what he took part

He was his mother's son
  in so many ways
But he was an individual
  his mother proudly would say

America watched him grow up
  he was our Royalty
The Prince of Camelot —
  son of the Kennedys

Never was nor will be anyone like him
  John-John was America's son
Playing under daddy's desk
  is when our love affair begun

He showed his greatest strength
   when his mother passed away
His chiseled cheeks would tighten
   at the grave he prayed

We rejoiced in his marriage
   to Carolyn, his beautiful wife
She was his soul mate
   now together for eternal life

I'm sure the angels were singing
   when his parents greeted him there
He'd introduce his wife and Lauren
   hugs and kisses they'd share

There's Grandma Rose and Grandpa Jo
   he'd excitedly would say
His brother Patrick, he never knew
   he'd meet on that day

The words of John's father
   are haunting to me
As he spoke of comparison
   of our bodies and the sea

"We have in our veins
   the same % of salt as in the ocean
Salt is in our blood, sweat and tears
   which ties us to the ocean

We go back to the sea —
   whether it is to watch or sail —
We go back from whence we came"
   His son, the ocean prevailed

Two Angels Watching Over You

Today I said a special prayer
for the parents of Carolyn and Lauren Bessette
They have faced the Greatest Pain —
one they will never forget

July 17, 1999
  was the tragic day
Their two beautiful daughters
  would suddenly vanish away

Two women in their prime of life
  successful in different ways
Lauren in the business field
  Carolyn a model on the runway

The pain must've been unbearable
  for these parents who loved them so
Questioning — Why, God, Why??
  really need to know!!

The answers don't seem to come
  as all of us can say
We all are still asking —
  why our child went away

Like most, I first blamed God
  but I know down deep inside
Our Heavenly Father loves us —
  He doesn't make us cry

There are many reasons
  that take away our babies
If we try to figure it out —
  it could drive us crazy

God gives us a free will —
  to make our own choices
It is Satan — too often
  drives us off our courses

Their loss was over-shadowed
  by the death of John Kennedy
The beloved husband of Carolyn
  Son of the famous family

It must've broken your heart
  to see them so shun
The media so insensitive
  as though John the only one

They were your shinning stars
  you lost, not one — but two
They were young and beautiful
  now their lives were through

There is no quick fix
  to take away the pain
Only God can give you peace
  your strength, He'll help regain

My walk with Christ
  has definitely helped me through
I'll see my son again
  your daughters you can too

If Jesus is your Lord and Savior
  have no doubts my friends
You will be with Carolyn and Lauren
  when your life also ends ...

Leo Lion

Leo was, without a doubt, the best friend anyone could have, male or female. I first met him at the local lounge where he bartended and worked with my three roommates. He had a great sense of humor and loved to be with people as I did. We hit it off immediately and became friends from that first day of meeting. I thought he was pretty cute but it was his personality that drew me to him. I have numerous, funny stories I could share about Leo but I'll start with one of my favorites.

We often went out to party together, with a group of friends, and one night he had his sister, Debbie, with him. She had heard a lot about me from her brother and I sensed a little jealousy over our friendship. She, being the only girl in their family, was very close to her brother and wasn't too anxious to share him.

As we were walking into a club, I complimented Debbie on her antique looking purse she was carrying and asked her where she got it. In a snobbish tone, she replied, "Oh! Thank you. I think I got it for 50." Leo started cracking up laughing but I had no idea why. Of course, Debbie made it sound like she paid $50.00 for it when actually she got it at a garage sale for 50 cents. She was trying to impress me, Leo told me later and didn't want to tell me she got it at a garage sale. Now that was funny! She didn't know I was Queen of Thrift! Leo knew but was laughing so hard he couldn't stop long enough to tell her. Later through the years, we had many laughs about that first meeting and Debbie and I have remained friends to this day.

One of the things Leo and I chuckled about for many years was the fact that I had a mad crush on him, when we first met, and so did one of my best girlfriends. After a few drinks one night, my friend, Tondra and I got into a heated argument over who Leo liked the most. Leo got a good laugh as he revealed to me that he preferred men over women. I did suspect it but didn't want it to be true, thus I pursued my feelings for him. We all laughed for a long time about our cat fight over him. Tondra and I remained good friends and actually I think it brought us even closer.

It broke my heart when Leo first became ill. I had suspected AIDS but I waited until he told me before I let my emotions flow. I offered to let him move into my house and I would take care of him but being the caring person he was, he refused and announced he was moving to California, He didn't want to be a burden on his mother or any of the people he loved, including me. "I don't want you to see me when it gets really bad," he said. He had been around others who died from this terrible disease and it wasn't easy to watch someone you love, decay before your eyes. We kept in touch regularly and I knew when he didn't call or answer my calls that he wasn't doing too well.

By this time, I had found my way back to the Lord and I would pray for and with my Leo Lion (my nickname for him). I talked about the love Jesus had for him, for all His children, no matter who or how we live. Jesus hates the sin, not the sinner, I'd say. Leo did know that Jesus was his Lord and Savior and he knew living a gay life was not the will of God. Leo assured me of his love for God, as he knew that was what I feared about his death. I'm so glad we talked about this, to give me peace of mind, since I feel he did ask for God's forgiveness and I will see my Leo Lion in eternal happiness in the Lord's Kingdom, in Heaven.

His strong pain lasted a short time and I was so grateful to God for taking him "home," the day before my birthday, November 4th. We had a beautiful ceremony at the park where I read his farewell poem and others read their words of love. We let go of dozens of balloons with words we sent floating up to tell him of our love and our missing his caring, loving self.

I miss my Leo Lion very much but I thank God for the years I had him for my best buddy. Sometimes I think what a great sense of humor our Lord has, taking him home the day before my B-Day, as He knows how bad my memory is, it was the only way I could remember the actual date of his death—or should I say rebirth. Six months later, my son Raymond died, on June 9th, one day before Leo's sister, Debbie's birthday. We always remembered to call each other on these dates.

Leo was in my life but a few short years, but that friendship was stronger than any that I have ever known. I look at his pictures and laugh, thinking how we'd drink our WHITE RHINE WINE, and how we would laugh so hard mocking that name that we could hardly ask for it in the stores. Probably because we had already had a few toddies. That was all before I came back to the Lord and had given up the booze and that life style. I'd also think of the serious times we shared and how we helped each other through the difficult times. Leo knew I didn't approve of the gay lifestyle, thus he never talked about it to me, although he knew I was there for him for whatever reason.

He was such a wonderful friend and I miss him so very much. I believe he was there to welcome my Raymond home when he died. I am glad because Ray thought Leo was the greatest—so do I.

A Treasure More Worthy Than Gold ... Your Friendship!!!

I've been searching, searching,
   for the right words to say
I think of my Leo
   every night and day

The memories of the yesteryears
   bring laughter to my heart
The tears that we shed
   were also a part

You are a friend —
   like no other —
Not sister, not brother,
   nor even a lover

You'd never question
   when I was wrong
But always there
   a friend so strong

Our quiet talks
   into the night
On my problems
   you'd shed a light

Your wisdom, strength
   a blessing to me
Opening my eyes
   to the wrongs you'd see

I love you, my Leo
  I pray for what's best
You're in God's hands now,
  He'll do the rest!!

Your friendship Leo
  is my greatest treasure
For you've given me
  so much pleasure

One can't buy
  a gift like this
A warm hug —
  a friendly kiss

I miss you my Leo
  but I'll never forget
The greatest friend
  I've ever had yet

My prayers are for you
  each night and day
Have mercy, dear Lord
  on Leo, I pray

Just call on Jesus, Leo
  confess your belief in Him
He'll be with you
  through the bitter end

He'll ease your pain
  He'll forgive you your sins
He'll bring you home
  for peace within

Let him suffer no more
  but "Thy Will Be Done"

Love & Miss You, my best friend

Memories of Love

How do you say goodbye
  to someone you love
When you know death is beckoning
  from beyond and above

Someone that you've cherished
  from the first day you met
You have to say goodbye —
  but NO—Not Yet!!!

You think of the yesteryears
  all the good times you had
You hear his warm laughter
  You're happy, — then you're sad

You remember all the gifts
  he lovingly gave to you
He picked them out special
  not just anything would do

What will I do now
  when I feel alone and blue
Without my Leo Lion
  to help me pull through

He was always there
  to love and comfort me
He took away the rainstorms
  and brought sunshine to see

He left his beloved family
  his friends he loved so dear
They wouldn't see him suffer
  throughout his dying years

He thought it would be easier
  if he, was in another state
So we didn't see death's hand
  slowly pull him to his fate

That was my Leo Lion
  my very best friend
Always giving of himself
  from deep within

How do you say goodbye?
  I couldn't, you see,
This poem should've been written
  when he was here with me

I so often tried
  to put the words onto page
But tears clouded my eyes
  when I tried to say ...

"Goodbye, My Leo Lion" —
  the words choke inside,
So I never wrote them, —
  my farewell, I couldn't cry —

Some people treasure money,
  silver or gold, I'm told
My friend, Leo Lion
  was my treasure of gold

You can't buy true friendship
   not like, my Leo, — my friend,
He was there for me
   up to his tragic end

He'd comfort me in my sorrow
   even though he was in pain
He'd share his words of wisdom
   my perspective, I'd regain

This was my Leo Lion,
   Always putting others first
Even after the disease of aids
   on him was cursed

But with a friend like Leo,
   it wasn't necessary you see
He knew how I felt —
   how much he meant to me

I count myself blessed
   to have known him at all
A friend you could count on
   anytime you called

How do you say goodbye?
   you don't my friend,
I'll see you later, Leo Lion, —
   in heaven we'll meet again

Mason

The story of Mason's death is one of the saddest and most complex which I have personally been in touch with. Mason's mother, Malika (we call her Molly), came to my Bible class one Sunday with her neighbor (our Bible teacher, Lila) and told of her tragedy.

Molly is not a member of our church, nor is she a Christian, but I have no doubt that the Lord sent her to us. She actually had come to the church looking for someone she had heard of that could help her in her dilemma. She told us this heartbreaking, unbelievable story about her son, Mason.

Mason was in the Coast Guard and they sent him to Bosnia along with numerous others for a training of some sort. It was not mandatory but since they were offering a pay of $50,000 for six months, he decided to take up the offer.

This very handsome young man of twenty-nine was married to a beautiful lady named Phatima. They had two daughters, Mounia, age five, Sarah, age two, and a baby boy, Hakeem, who was just a few months old at that time.

Molly said neither she nor Phatima had heard from Mason in an unusually long time and they didn't know why. Upon trying to contact him, they were first told they never even had him listed in the "Army." (This was where he was assigned while over there.) After more persistence, they said he had run away (AWOL—absence without leave) and had no idea where he was. They had been looking for him quite some time. Molly was at her wit's end and in desperate need of help from anyone who could help her.

After much unwanted publicity all over the media, the service said they found him in Germany where he had committed suicide by hanging himself from a tree, with his hands tied behind his back. His senior officer said that he had told him he was having money problems so that must have been why he killed himself. Molly said that was 100% RIDICULOUS!

First of all, he had $10,000 in his savings and he'd have another $50,000 when he got back to the states from the service for volunteering to go over there. Besides that, he was not ever greedy for money. He also had too much to live for—his wife, three babies and numerous family and friends who loved him very much. He had absolutely no reason to even think of killing himself! Things just didn't add up and his devastated wife and mother were looking for answers that fit the puzzle.

To make this long story short, after tons of interviews from newspapers, the T.V. media and talking to attorneys, they got a few answers but not the right ones. After many headaches and years later, plus the disappearance of one of their attorneys, they had given up, at least at this time.

Since that time, Molly did learn of another young man who had very similar happenings to him and was also "found" dead by the Army, also in Germany, (which is where Molly and his mother were both born) one year before Mason's death and he too was from West Palm Beach, Florida, where Molly lives. His story was also published in many newspapers. She has also learned there are many other young men who have mysteriously disappeared or found dead later, all of which were said to have killed themselves.

Molly says she at least found some peace that her son was found but she will never believe that he committed suicide and neither will his wife! Neither will I. She has been offered to do a book and a movie but she turned them down as she just wanted it to be over. She holds no grudges against anyone and says she "knows her Mason is at peace and in a better place and will see him again one day.

Our Bible class keeps Molly and all of the family in our prayers to find the right answers, to give them final closure and I believe one day, they will.

Thy Will Be Done

There are no words fitting
　　that one can say to you
To try to ease the pain —
　　your family is going through

I also felt this pain
　　when my son passed away
It's been four years now
　　but seems like yesterday

"It's just not fair—
　　for your kids to die first!"
I shouted in anger —
　　as I felt my heart burst

My son was suffering —
　　which was a little easier for me
To let go of him —
　　of pain he'd be set free

I felt so empty —
　　and bitter inside —
WHY, God, WHY?
　　did my son have do die

Yes — I blamed God
　　for taking him away
I shouted angrily
　　when I tried to pray

Then I was sorry —
   for I knew deep within
God loved me
   He was my best friend

I am also His child
   He would never hurt me
Satan is the evil one
   the blame should go to he

I know your faith is different
   than the one that I know
I can only tell you
   that God loves you so

Without His strength and Love
   I couldn't handle my loss
God also knows your pain
   He gave the greatest cost

As a Christian, our beliefs —
   I'm very happy to say
We will see our sons again
   in Heaven where they stay

I know God loves your son
   as much as He loves mine
So be at peace to know
   Mason is with the Devine

It is we who suffer
   for we miss them so much
We'd love to hold our little boys
   to kiss and gentle touch

Until that day comes to us
  there's nothing we can do
Except ask God to strengthen us
  each day help us through

God loves you Malika
  and all your family
He will help you — If you ask
  this He guarantees ...

Paul

When I asked Madeline if she would like to write a little something about her son, Paul, she was reluctant at first, saying she wouldn't know what to write. "I'm not a writer," she said to me. "I would have no idea what you would want me to say." "Whatever you want to say, just say how you are feeling from your heart."

What you are about to read are the words of a hurting mother, after the loss of her son. I believe she reflected the pain, we, as parents would all write about She talks of how she just would like to scream at people—"That her son was dead!"—Didn't they know—or care?

It seemed disrespectful, unfair that everyone could just go on living—having a good time without my child here. That is what I use to think and want to say, even to complete strangers. I had seen a mother in a store with a small child, scolding or hitting him, and I would think, you might regret that one day. If that child dies, you would think, I should've treated him (or her) better. I shouldn't have. Now it's too late, he is gone; I just want to SCREAM!

I too, just wanted to sleep all day and hope that when I woke up it would have been just a nightmare—Raymond was still alive. I also thought the tears would never stop flowing. There were a few times I had to walk out of the stores, leaving baskets of items because everything I saw reminded me of my son and I couldn't stop the gushes of tears. It's been over seven years and I still say to myself and others that it is hard to believe that Ray is no longer here. I still see him watching his favorite T.V. shows and eating his favorite foods and yes, Madeline, I still sometimes question Why? Why? Why?

I am saying all of this to show you, the readers, that we are not alone in these types of thoughts. No, we are not going crazy, as we feel we are so often. Yes, it's okay to do all these things, as it is just part of the grieving, that we deserve and need to do. But trust me, dear friends, it will get better. We will still miss them, we will still cry, we will still yearn to hold and kiss them, but we will be able to breathe a little better than today. And yes, it is okay to be able to get up in the morning and go to bed at night, and even in between, without our child on our minds. It doesn't mean that we love them less or that we are going to forget about them, it just means we are finally starting our healing process.

This process will get better as the years go by, but just as Madeline's mom said, "We never get over it." If we did, there would be something wrong with us. Only God and time will help ease our pain. That's why it is said, "God never gives us anything which we can't handle." I know at first we think there is no way we will get through this but with God's help, it is a lot easier than without Him, from what I have seen.

August 7, 2001

Paul has been gone four months today. Losing a child is truly the most painful experience of my life and I still cannot imagine anything worse. At first, when Paul died, I couldn't believe I could go on functioning, only wanting to curl up in a ball in the corner of a closet; but life truly does go on no matter what happens in our world. I couldn't stop crying and I think I cried all the way home from Virginia. Whenever I am around people, I sometimes just want to shout, "Don't you know my son is dead, he died!"

The first few months, I felt like I would shatter into a million pieces. I cried everyday on the way home from work. I even lost it three times at work and cried. People say things that cut you to the quick. I don't think they mean to or even realize what they've done, but it still hurts.

By the third month, a kind of numbness sets in, you still hurt but in a different way. My mother said she still can't believe he's gone. She spent a lot of time with Paul through his childhood and lived with him as an adult. Her brother died when he was twenty-three and that was fifty-eight years ago. Mom says she still misses him, they were very close.

A friend of ours came over the day of Paul's service and he said his brother had died two years ago and a day doesn't go by that he doesn't think of him.

Paul is my last thought when I go to bed at night and my first thought when I awake. I prayed for him all his life to be protected and in God's Will. It's hard not to ask why?

I Have Called You By Your Name —
You Are Mine
Isaiah 43:1

The only thing worse for a Christian
   than losing a child my friend
Is not knowing if their child —
   was saved in the end

I know, Ed and Madeline
   this is how you felt
When your son's early death
   was so unfairly dealt

I know about your feelings yes,
   I knew them all too well
As I feared that my son,
   Raymond was damned for Hell

God knew of my fear
   for I cried it out each day
God in all His Mercy
   proved my Ray was saved

I believe that in God's Goodness
   He also showed this to you
By giving you time with Paul
   before his life was through

Not just to say your "farewells"
   but to share God's Mercy and Love
So that you both would know —
   he'd be with his Father above

Although Paul didn't say it verbally
   I believe his feelings were seen
When a tear moist his eye —
   saying Dad, —"I receive..."

Paul knew of your love for God
   as it was shown in the way you lived
Both of you sharing God's Love —
   always to others, you give

All parents want their child
   to be in Heaven with them
Which is why our Heavenly Father
   had his Son die for our sins

God knows your pain
   as He felt it too
As He watched His Son in agony
   die for me and you

Mary's heart was also broken
   as she watched her dying Son
Beaten unrecognizable
   for our souls He had won ...

Tomorrow we all celebrate
   Christians most triumphed day
When Jesus Christ Resurrects
   Halleluiah!! Eternal Life we pray

This Easter, Ed and Madeline
   no doubt will be more profound
As you think of your Savior
   and your son — year round

Did Christ not leave his ninety-nine
   to find that one lost sheep
Would He not do this for your son
   before his final sleep

You have been good stewards
   God will honor your faithfulness
He gave Paul time to accept Christ
   his long illness was a Bless

Jesus Loves me this I know
   for the Bible tells me so
God has said to tell you—
   "BE STILL AND KNOW" ...

Ryan... Love and Prayer Can Conquer All

Helen had been a friend of mine for a couple of years when she told me about the birth of her twin grandsons, Ryan and James. She and the parents had been so excited about their forthcoming but their joy quickly turned into fear and sadness at their birth.

Both of their precious gifts were afflicted with a disease, which the doctors had no hope for either child. Their hearts felt like they had been stabbed when just two short hours after their arrival, Ryan quickly passed away. Through their darkness was a ray of hope and light as baby James was still breathing. His mother, Christina, was determined not to let the hand of death snatch away her second son. With God's help, she knew all things were possible and began to fight for his life.

Helen was telling me this story because she wanted me to write her a poem, expressing her gratitude and admiration for the love she had shown through the years for this helpless child. After I had heard the story, I immediately thought of the Biblical story of David and Goliath. Christina certainly had her Giant to fight but because of her endless devotion and love, James surpassed the minute expectation any of the doctors had given him. Helen said she praised her son, Rene, in his contribution in the care taking of his son, but it was Christina who fought day and night to nurse him back to health.

God also blessed them with a healthy, beautiful baby girl, who has helped James to grow up faster, as in someway he knew he was the older brother and he had to help his little sissy. Helen told me at the time I wrote their poem what a big difference baby Noelle had made in James' life. She was born on December 1st, which is why she was given the name associated with Christmas, which means JOY, and that is what she had given to all of them, especially her big brother, James.

I haven't seen Helen in many years and I have no update on James but I have a gut feeling he is doing just great thanks to his loving parents who refused, like David, to let the Goliath beat them! I also know (for I was one) who sent lots of prayers up to God, asking for a healing on their child. I have no doubt "Dr." Jesus had a big healing hand on this child and a special angel named Ryan watching over him.

I remember saying many years ago that I didn't believe I could ever handle a child who was terminally ill or handicapped. I somehow told myself then that God never gives us anything we can't handle. Those words came back to me as I watched my son dying. How true it is. As in Christina's and Rene's case, I believe that although their children's disease wasn't given to them by God, He gave the parents the strength to get through it.

Love and Prayer Can Conquer All

Many blessings are given to us
  from our Lord up above
But the greatest that he gives
  is a child made out of love

There is nothing more rewarding
  than that day of birth
All the riches in this world
  can't buy this child's worth

When God sends a "special" child
  who needs extra love and care
He will choose a mother
  to no other can compare

When James and Ryan were born
  to Christina and Rene
They were blessed twice
  on this wonderful day

But a shadow overcame them
  it was evident to see
They were "special children"
  who were helpless as could be

The doctors had no hope
  they said nothing could be done
But the hearts of Christina and Rene
  had already been won

They were their flesh and blood
  they couldn't give up now
They would help them survive ...
  Someway ... Somehow!!

God in all His Mercy
  took Ryan home to stay
He left his loving parents
  In two short hours that day

Christina was more determined
  to save her only son
With the help of God
  she knew victory could be won

It would take lots of patience
  and extra care and love
But nothing was impossible
  with help from above

She worked with James daily
  and sometimes through the night
This disease was his Goliath
  and as David, she would fight!!

A child is like a flower
  they need nourishment to grow
And when that child is special
  more love needs to flow

That's why God in all his wisdom
  chose Christina to be there
Because his "special child"
  would need the best of care

Not all mothers are capable
   to give of their life,
To be the best of mothers
   and a loving, giving wife

James has beaten the odds
   and he is five years old
Doing things he'd never do
   as they had been told

He is still blossoming
   with each passing day
His parents are so proud
   and give thanks as they pray

All the love you've given
   to this beautiful child
Is rewarded ten-fold
   when he looks at you and smiles

But this wouldn't have been possible
   without a mother such as you
You have made his rainbows,
   out of the gloom

Children have a special sense
   unknown to you and me
A way of reaching others,
   it's called innocence, you see

Songs of joy will be ringing
   from the Nadeau house this year
For you have many reasons
   to sing Christmas cheers!!

One must never question
   the way things are to be
Just pray for strength and guidance
   to conquer triumphantly

For James has been a blessing
   in these five wonderful years
No one can take that away
   the memories you hold so dear

You were also blessed
   by having a brother for James
Now he's one of God's angels
   from Heaven he will reign

Ryan is James' guardian angel,
   always by his side
Protecting him from danger
   being his daily guide

And as of December the 1st
   Ryan's job has doubled
Now he has sister Noelle,
   to keep out of trouble

Noelle is also a blessing
   for big brother James
They will help each other
   by playing learning games

So on this Birthday of Jesus,
   I though it appropriate, you see
To tell my daughter-in-law
   how "special" you are to me

We just want to thank you
  we love you very much
For giving our little James
  your tender care and touch...

Boop – Rusty

Rusty had been a friend of my son, Raymond, for many years. I remember seeing him at Ray's funeral, and how lost he looked. Boop as a very quiet and shy guy, who kept pretty much to himself. He was the complete opposite of Raymond which is why he probably enjoyed Ray's outgoing and silly ways with people.

I worked with him at a diner where he was the chef. He showed his real ability to cook at his family's steakhouse, which was considered the best restaurant around for many, many years. Boop was their head chef and deservingly so. Ray's favorite was the homemade barrenaise sauce, he always requested EXTRA so he could pour it on his potato, steak and just sop it up with their delicious bread. Boop always took good care of his buddy, especially when Ray was bed-ridden and I'd pick the food up to take home to him.

Boop was the oldest of two sisters and one brother. He also had two step brothers from his step-dad, who owned the restaurant.

My kids grew up with the boys and we all knew each other from another lounge that they owned and were they worked. Of all the kids, Boop was the one who partied the least, other than his beer and little "pot." The reason I am saying this is he was another of our kids lost to drugs, from an overdose. I had been out of the partying scene (thank God) and had lost touch with that side of the world, but I was shocked as was all of his family. They had no idea he was doing hard drugs. The girls also had been out of that scene and said if either of their brothers would do this, it would be the youngest, since he was still the partyer.

I think Boop was very lonely and he could have been a depressed young man. I know he had no girlfriend and for a long time had been in search of his "Miss Right." I don't know why he didn't have one as he was like my Ray in that field. He showered them with love and gifts and did pretty much whatever they wanted. Boop's last girlfriend hurt him very much, as they were engaged to get married and for no reason she left him. I know he was crushed and I don't think he ever had a serious relationship after that.

It's sad we don't know this about our kids before it is too late but usually they aren't living at home with us and never show their loneliness, especially to their mothers.

This was the second son Rusty's mother had lost and needless to say, she was in total denial. Her first son had died in a car crash about fifteen years before but as anyone who has lost a child knows, it still feels like yesterday. I can't imagine burying two of my kids and I pray to God I never have to know that pain. My heart broke as I watched this family grieve over the loss of their loving, caring, generous young man who had made the mistake of using drugs to kill his pain—and that it did.

This is the family I had been given a poem from someone in my Bible class when I spilled the coffee on it and as I wiped it up, it formed the rose that looked like Ray's rose. The one who gave it to them was trying to tell them how the Lord had helped them through the loss of their son. They had also known this family for years before they had stopped their drinking and gave their life to Christ. They wanted them to know that they don't know how they could have gotten through it if they didn't know the Lord.

About a year after Boop's death, one of his sisters had asked me how I got through Ray's death. Had I gone through therapy or a group of some kind or what? Only by the Grace of God had I been able to handle it through the years, I told her. Yes, we Christians have the same pain, but we also have hope that one day we will be with our kids in Heaven one day as we believe that Jesus Christ is our Lord and Savior.

I am still praying for this family to come to know the Lord. I do know that there were a lot of Boop's friends there who were still partying and I heard them talking afterwards about maybe it was time to give up the drugs before something happened to them. I pray that they or at least one of them quit. At least Boop's death wouldn't be in vain.

We miss this gentle person, with the silly nickname of Boop, but he will remain in our hearts with loving memories.

To Know Him Was to Love Him

Mothers think that giving birth
  is the greatest pain by far
Until that child, precedes them in death
  and we lose that shining star

Then we know, the greatest of pain
  too difficult to explain
Your heart is "truly breaking"
  for your child that death proclaimed

We ask WHY? Why must this be—
  then blame and guilt sets in
Maybe I could've — should've — done this —
  then his life may not have end

I know the pain that you feel
  for I felt it too
But I know now, deep in my heart
  there was nothing I could do

They were no longer, our "little boys"
  they had their own free will
Right or Wrong, they would choose
  as they climbed the aging hill

We all have made mistakes
  for which we usually pay
I'm so sorry that your son
  paid in the worst way

No one knew better than God
  what was in Rusty's heart
I'm sure he made his peace
  before his life did part

So you be at peace, Jeannie
  God loved your child too
I'm sure you'll see your child again
  when God beckons you

He also knows a parents pain
  for He also felt this too
When he gave His only Son
  to die for me and you

Christ stretched out His arms for us
  so reach out now to Him
Only He can give you peace
  way down deep within

You WILL HAVE YOUR "Boop Days"
  feeling depressed and blue
Just remember the good times
  that he shared with you

Think about his friendly smile
  he gave to one and all
No matter friend or stranger
  on Boop, you could call

His voice was soft spoken
  and quiet in his ways
Never gossiped about others
  throughout his days

His heart was so caring
   for everyone he knew
Especially for Jeannie and Curtis
   he loved both of you

You are a good mother, Jeannie
   your love always shown through
The love from your kids is obvious
   when it comes to you

The same goes for Curtis
   who raised them as his own
Helping out in the businesses
   their gratitude and love shown

As for brother Robbie,
   he also was his friend
Doing for each other —
   through thick and thin

Like any other siblings
   they also shared fights
But were buddies again
   before the end of night

The pain of his loss will linger
   for Pam and Cindy too
It will take prayers for strength
   to help them pull through

As it will for Ralph and Vern
   and all of his family and friends
But they know that their life —
   was made better by knowing him

"It is better to have loved and lost
   than, never to have loved at all" —
This saying has a new meaning —
   when it comes to Boop for us all —

Close your eyes, Jeannie —
   feel the beat of your heart
That's your son close to you
   each day when you start

Stephanie

Stephanie was a beautiful one year old baby girl, who was deeply loved by her parents and older brother, Devon. At the time of this terrible accident, I believe Devon was only three or four years old.

I was working in a little diner when one of the waitresses told me what had happened to this family. I realized I knew them when she described them as both being young, very pleasant, and having two beautiful children. They made their living by entertaining. Steve played the piano and Angie sung in the local, nice lounges. Their pride and love for their two children was evident when they brought them to our restaurant. It was also obvious how much Devon loved being big brother to baby sister, as he tried to help her with her bottle and passy, giving her hugs and kisses. What a beautiful family they were together.

When Sharon told me about what happened, I was in tears for the pain I knew they had to be going through. Little Devon was playing with Stephanie as he usually would do. He was hiding and would call her name, so she would come looking for him as they had done so many times before. Only this time, it was to become an unexpected tragedy. Devon was hiding behind the television, which was sitting on a table, when his baby sissy, came in and pulled on the scarf under the television. Suddenly, the whole table tumbled over on top of her little body and crushed her.

Needless to say, the mother was just in shock when she saw what had happened to her baby. Devon was too young to understand that his sissy was dead, but later, Angie and Steve had to try to tell him in a way he could possibly understand. Even though he was so young, Devon was deeply hurt at what he said was his fault. They eventually had to seek professional help for him to get him to realize it was just a freak accident.

I haven't seen Angie and Steve in many years but I think about them often and pray they have all come to peace with their loss. I know that they are still in the music industry since I have seen their names on the marquees around town.

Devon would be a young man now and I especially pray he has forgiven himself for something that wasn't his fault in the first place.

An Angel in the Heavens

When we lose someone we love
   we can't explain the pain
It hurts so deep within our hearts
   we feel life can't be the same

But somehow Steve and Angie
   you'll make it through these days
God will give you strength
   just ask Him when you pray

The memory of Stephanie
   will always be with you
The love that you shared
   will continue, life through

She gave you so much happiness
   in just one short year
But that happiness is yours
   to cherish forever dear

Some people aren't that lucky
   for they've never had a child
They've never had the pleasure
   of seeing that little smile

Is it better to have loved and lost
   than never to have loved at all
I think the answer is yes
   as her memory, you recall

You'll see your little girl again
   when God beckons you Home
You will hug and kiss her
   through Heaven's land you'll roam

Until that glorious reunion
   Stephanie will always be there
She'll be your Guardian Angel
   protecting you everywhere

She'll watch over brother, Devon
   when he goes out to play
She'll be by his side
   through the night and day

Only God knows the answer
   why Stephanie had to go
So pray to Him for strength
   someday He'll let you know —

The Day From Hell

The day from Hell was the first thought that came to mind when I heard of this most tragic accident. I never had met this family but I felt their grief, their pain. One of my friends had kids who went to school with the three children who had died but I first heard it on the news. The shock threw me into a rage of tears. My heart went out for the hurting parents and for the uncle who was driving the car. How could this happen, I found myself repeating over and over?

The three kids were riding home from church in their uncle's car when a tire blew out. The car went out of control and into a lake, trapping all three children into a watery grave. Only the uncle had managed to crawl out of the window but was unable to reach his little nephew and nieces. By the time help had arrived, it was too late for Andrew, Phoena and Shawn. The ambulance took the dazed driver to the hospital and the authorities contacted the parents of the drowned victims. They were all from Haiti and the father was a preacher at the church where they had attended the morning of the accident.

The first question came to mind of those that I talked to was WHY? Why would this happen to a man of God—WHY would God allow it to happen? Only God can answer that question and only God can get the parents through their Hell on earth. The title for their poem couldn't be any more appropriate as I have no doubt this pain was caused by Satan himself, straight from the pits of HELL! What great pleasure for him to see the parents of these servants of God, by taking all three of their children at the same time, in hopes that they would lose their faith and love for their God by blaming Him. As I said, I do not know this family nor do I know what is going on in their life since, but I pray, nor do I believe that Satan won their souls.

As of this date, I haven't been able to obtain any further information on them but I do continue praying for God to give them the strength they need to endure this pain every day of their lives. As I stated in the poem, I can't begin to imagine what it would be like to lose more than one child at one time.

I thought of a family in my home town in Ohio who lost three kids out of four at one time. They were all teenagers and were leaving to go to school when the car accident occurred killing all of them. The only reason the one wasn't in the car is because she wasn't ready and told them to go without her and she would catch a ride from someone else. It just so happened that she was dating my brother at the time and he was very devastated when he heard about it and grateful she wasn't in the car too. I didn't know the family well except for the fact that they use to eat in a German restaurant where I worked, when I lived in Ohio. This all happened long before my son had died but even then I had great passion for this family's pain. I know that the family were good Christians and with lots of support from numerous family members and friends and relying on strength from the God they loved and depended on, they got through their fire, one day at a time.

As I write and think of the pain these parents suffered losing three children, I can't help thinking of the parent or parents who purposely killed their children, like Susan Smith, who let her two beautiful little boys drown when she sent them strapped in her car to their watery grave as they pleaded for her to help them. The whole country was in shock when they learned that it was their own mother who killed her precious gifts from God. Why would a mother kill her own little helpless children? We know in Susan's case, it was because she wanted the love a man that she didn't have and thought it was because he didn't want a ready-made family and if she got rid of them, he would love her. We know that was her excuse but what, or should I say, who really caused her to do such a horrible crime?

Once again, I say it was the prince of this world who controls all evils and brings them about. I recently heard of two more women who murdered their kids because of some sickness they both had, according to the findings of medical doctors. The one mother drowned her five kids in the bathtub. I couldn't say what her illness was but I believe they both were bipolar, which caused a deep depression and they do crazy, uncontrollable things such as this. It is hard for us to believe but it does happen. Her husband said he completely forgave her as he knows she is sick and had been for some time. Why then didn't she have help before she did this horrifying crime?

I am not sitting in judgement as it is not us they will face on Judgement Day, but I do pray for these women to get the help they so desperately need. I pray if anyone of you know of someone in this same situation that you get them help before it is too late for them or their kids.

The Day from Hell

There's not a word in Webster
  that can possibly describe
The way you both felt
  when your three children died

To lose one — I know is painful —
  two — I'd be in denial my friend —
Three —I just can't imagine —
  I feel my world would end

Why would this happen??!! —
  to this godly woman and man
They love their Lord and Saviour
  they preach on God's earthy land

Satan is the prince of this land
  as all of us well know
He causes us agony
  that deeply hurts us so

He wants us to blame God
  as most of us will do
Forgetting that it's Satan —
  who wants to destroy you

Our God is a loving God —
  doesn't cause us pain
He will give us strength —
  although it's Him we blame

God knows the pain you feel
   for He felt it too
His son died in excruciating pain
   out of love for me and you

As in the poem, "Footprints" —
   when a tragedy you face
God will carry you through
   with His amazing grace

If you will close your eyes —
   sit very, very still
God's loving arms —
   around you, you'll feel

He will give you comfort —
   this I guarantee
I felt the pain as you
   and He comforted me

When you have those days —
   you feel you just can't breathe
God is the breath of life
   give it up to He

When your arms ache to hold them
   do as I do friend
Close your eyes and vision
   feel their heartbeats within

I envision my son in heaven
   he's having so much fun
Singing with God's angels
   with the animals he runs

Oh how he loves it there
  he has no worries or fear
The best reason of all
  Jesus is always near

Why did this accident happen
  why all three you say —
Us mortals just can't answer
  but God will one day

One thing is for certain
  Christians are Satan's market
He already has the non-believer
  to destroy our faith — he targets

Satan may have won this battle
  but don't let him win the war
Tell him you're a child of God —
  only Him you worship and adore

Your day of GLORY will come
  you'll meet on God's heavenly land
Andrew — Pheona and Shawn
  will greet you hand in hand ...

From a Lemon to Lemonade

It's been so many years ago
  since Adam went away
But your pain is as strong
  as though were yesterday

Oh, yes, I know that pain ...
  I know it all too well...
When my son, Raymond, died
  I felt that pain of hell

Only Satan can cause that evil...
  that took your son from you
Only God can ease the pain ...
  each day help you through

You are a blessing, John ...
  for you've turned this evil around
Your love for Adam is your lifestyle
  VERB ... not a noun ...

Although you miss him terribly
  rejoice in knowing my friend
You can be with your son ...
  when your time on earth ends

I know you've made him proud
  as he watches from above
Dedicated to helping others
  who also lost their love

I see Adam, as God's angel
 aiding in your drive
Helping all the children ...
 he comforts as they cry

Out of the Love of Jesus
 Adam's body, has been made new
Out of the Love of Jesus
 eternal Life is offered to you

If you feel an invisible kiss
 softly upon your cheek
Adam's saying, "Dad, I love you ...
 for me, please don't weep

I am safe and happy here ...
 with my heavenly Dad
Know Jesus, as your Lord and Savior
 this will make me glad!!

Thank you for making lemonade ...
 out of the "Lemon," given you
My death has not been in vain ...
 because of the both of you ...

Someday we will be together ...
 you can hold me in your arms
We know only peace here, mom and dad
 away from Satan's harm ....

A Mother's Broken Heart

When a baby dies shortly —
  after he or she is born
I will guarantee —
  that mother's heart is torn

Although you lived a day or two
  I knew you well she'd say
We spent many months together
  we bonded every day

I planned so carefully
  as I anxiously await
Counting the months and days
  for that far away date

Your bedroom looks so beautiful
  with fancy bows and frills
And lots of dollies and teddy bears ...
  my heart leaped with thrills

My anxious moment finally arrived
  it was time to say hello
Time to hold you in my arms ...
  but a problem I didn't know

I held you my little Angel...
  to say hello and goodbye
I felt the life drain from you
  my heart broke as I cried

I felt so empty inside ...
  figuratively and not
My arms ached longing ...
  to hold my little tot

When I looked into your room
  my eyes blurred with tears
I rocked your little dolly
  pretending it's my Angel dear

How dare they say I didn't know you
  because you lived a short while
I knew you from head to toe ...
  especially your beautiful smile

Our closeness was immeasurable
  as I laid silently each night
I felt your every heart beat
  I envisioned holding you tight

I dreamt of you daily ...
  of all the tomorrows to come
I can't wait for this child, I'd say,
  we will have so much fun

Never belittle this pain
  a mother is going through
Even if he never lived ...
  outside of her womb ...

For "he" lived within her
  she knew "him" so well...
Now she deeply grieves ...
  feeling the pain of "HELL"

It doesn't take a life time
to love this bundle of joy
You love them from conceivement
this baby girl or boy

Angel wasn't my only child
that I lost this way
The hand of death also swept...
my Sarah and Thomas away

I now have three children ...
Tony, Rachel and Mary
I prayed for their good health
the nine months I carried

I love them all deeply
but there's a hole in my heart
For my three beautiful babies
so quick to depart

I know they all are angels ...
watching over me
I'll meet them all again ...
in God's heavenly regime ...

God's Time Clock

Often we face tragedies
  we just don't understand
Angrily we will shout
  for God's helping hand

I know that's the way you felt —
  when Anthony went away
Asking — where was my God —
  on this tragic day

I know — for that was me
  six years ago too
When I faced the "Deepest of Pain"
  any parent will go through

My Raymond was thirty-one
  but still my baby boy
It seemed like only yesterday
  I held my bundle of joy

No matter how long or short
  you spent with your child
He stole your heart from the start
  made living worthwhile

Yes, I know how you felt
  which is why I say —
For Mother, Father and family
  I promise to pray

I know — now — it wasn't God
  who took our child away
I have peace in knowing —
  with Him, they now stay

Someday we will hold them
  like we use to do
Because of the love of Jesus
  who died for me and you

His Mother also knew this pain
  as she watched through teary eyes
Her son suffering so much
  when He was crucified

God Never Deserts us
  He is always there
He carries us through the fires
  because He deeply cares

We don't know why things happen
  but we must do our best
To turn the bad into good
  put our bitterness to rest

You have two little blessings
  Kanealoha and Mickale too
They were God's gifts —
  to help you get through

God blessed you both again
  with two more shining stars
With Big Brother Anthony
  protecting from afar

He'll be their special Angel
  Natasha and Jamma too
Someday he'll welcome them home
  as he will each of you ...

Blessed Are They That Mourn For They Shall Be Comforted
Matt. 5-4

There is singing in the heavens today
  The angels shout with joy
They will welcome another —
  Of God's "little boys"

David wasn't a child to us
  but to God he still is
Everyone of you here
  are one of His kids

To his Mom and Dad
  he was a handsome young man
But he was still their "little boy"
  the best on God's earthly land

To his daughter, Juliana,
  her daddy is 12 feet tall
Now he will be her special angel
  to catch her when she falls

To his beautiful Michelle
  an emptiness will be in her life
Oh, how she loves her David
  And loved being his wife

To Sissy, Gretchen, he says,
   take care of Mom and Dad —
And remember the good times
   in our childhood we had

I'll be waiting for you Grandpa
   with Grandma by my side
We will welcome you "HOME"
   with our arms opened wide

Help take care of my Juliana
   please, Donna and Shane
I thank you with all my heart
   for letting Michelle take my name

To all my family and friends
   I have just one request
Remember me with love —
   and CELEBRATE my final rest

For I have not left you
   I'm just gone physically
We will be together again
   for all of eternity ...

A Precious Gem Still Shining

The first time you held your child
  your heart jumped with joy
You dreamt about the future
  for your little girl or boy

I'm sure when Don and Diane
  held Debbie the first time
Never thought that life
  would be so unkind

You envision their first step
  and their first day at school
Think how you will teach her
  God's Golden Rules

Oh how beautiful she'll be
  in her special prom dress
She's bound to stand out
  above all the rest

How proud you both will be
  on her graduation day
Thank you God for sending
  this special one our way

Tears of happiness flow
  as you envision your "Precious Gem'
Daddy walking her down the aisle
  and hands her over to him

How excited you'll be
  when she too gives birth
All these thoughts pass through
  about this bundle of worth

But all these dreams were shattered
  that terrible tragic night
When the hand of death
  crept in and took flight

Coming back from Orlando
  where she cheered for her team
An accident happened quickly
  scaring all the teens

The van went flying and flipping
  out the window Debbie flew
She's the only one who died
  the other seven lived through

The cheerleaders were stunned
  they didn't understand why
Why weren't we killed
  why did only Debbie die

ONLY God knows for sure
  ONLY He can truly say
ONLY Debbie was a Christian
  ONLY she — HEAVEN would gain

Debbie's parents were sickened —
  but they had peace within
Their daughter knew the Lord
  now she was with him

"Sorry about your LOSS,"
  her parents heard people say
My daughter is Not LOSS
  she just changed her address that day

We know where Debbie is
  her dad tenderly said —
She's alive and happy —
  she is NOT dead

She will live for eternity
  as will we someday
She will welcome us home
  Hallelujah —we will say

Debbie had been a witness for God
  to all her non-Christian peers
She shared His unselfish love
  throughout her 15 years

She sung His Glory and Praises
  when they went to Baltimore
She was one of the youths —
  in the First Baptist Choir tour

Debbie was ahead of her time
  wanting to do signing for the deaf
It wasn't in her church then
  but is now, since she has "left"

Debbie's "RE-BIRTH" into Heaven
  was special in brother, David's heart
The day before his 9th birthday —
  is when she would depart

He would miss his big Sis deeply
　　but her memories he'd treasure
They celebrate their "BIRTH" day together
　　a gift you just can't measure

What Satan meant for evil that day
　　God turned into good
Debbie's death won many souls
　　as God knew it would

A "Celebration of Life" was held
　　to honor this "Precious Gem"
Her love for Christ kept giving
　　after her life did "end"

The Church was filled with loved ones
　　many from Debbie's school —
Who gave their life to Christ
　　that making Satan the losing fool!

God knows how you were hurting
　　as He watched you from above
So He sent you Stacy
　　to "adopt" in love

No one can take Debbie's place
　　we all know this is true
But what a blessing Stacy's been
　　these many years through

A special student in Don's class
　　put her in your heart
Although she lives in Michigan
　　it doesn't keep you apart

You both have been her blessing
  As she needed your love too
Now you give it to her kids
  it multiplies each year through

That's the way God's love is
  It keeps multiplying ten fold
Until that GLORIOUS day comes
  When Debbie again you'll hold

God's Light Will Brighten Your Tomorrows

I know your hearts are breaking,
   since Doug has gone away
I felt that way also
   when I lost my Ray

I wish I had a solution
   I'd throw it in the air
Taking away the pain
   of parents everywhere

For there is no deeper pain
   this I guarantee
When a child dies suddenly
   his parents he precedes

It feels like a knife stabbing
   way down deep inside
When will this nightmare end
   in agony you cry

There is no quick fix
   I am sorry to say
But I recommend daily
   go to God an pray

He understands this pain
   for He felt it too
When He watched His Son, Jesus, die
   out of love for me and you

God has given me so much peace
   as the days gone by
Although I first blamed Him
   when my Raymond died

I knew down deep
   it wasn't God's fault
For we choose our own road —
   I was always taught

For years, I traveled the wrong road
   doing many stupid things
Searching for that happiness
   that booze and drugs won't bring

Ray's death gave me back my life
   this may be hard to understand
It gave me a reality check
   what was I doing on God's land

My life is really a mess, I thought
   than I fell to my knees
Please, God help me ...
   tearfully I'd plead

Now I've found that happiness
   through God's Amazing Grace
I try to ease the pain
   that other parents face

For God has given me a gift
   as He has to all of you
Use it to help others
   before your life is through

I know not why, Matty and Chuck
  before us, our sons died
I know — not to question —
  someday He'll tell us why

I've learned to put my trust in God
  Ray's death is not in vain
God has carried me through the storm
  my strength, I've regained

He will do this for all of you
  "just ask and you shall receive"
This is what our Lord and Saviour
  has promised us, you see

Maybe their dying young is telling us
  we don't choose when or where
When the hand of death reaches out
  it is not always fair

The only thing sure about death
  is death is sure, my friend
We will all meet our Maker
  when our time ends

So don't let Doug's death
  be in vain too
Maybe it's a wake-up call
  for some of you

Often when we lose a child
  we ask, "Did I do my best?"
Believe me, Marty and Chuck
  you can put that fear to rest

I know how much Doug loved you
   as do Dave and Donny too
They always spoke highly —
   of the both of you

Everyone who knows the Greens
   give the "p's" high praise
Love flowed from your house
   with each child you raised

All the kids in the "hood"
   felt at home at the Greens
I know that my Raymond
   thought you both SUPREME!

Doug's family and friends will miss him
   his son, Nicholus, will too
Just remember the good times
   you shared the years through ...

Ennis Has Found the Best Friend

HELLO Friend!
  you know me not...
Nor do I you
  except in pain, we both go through

For the hand of death
  cheated us both
Of our greatest wealth
  un-measurable in worth

We know not why —
  our sons left so soon
Why he wasn't even ...
  full bloom — full bloom ...

Although we weep
  at the thought of him
We pray, Dear God ...
  let this pain end ...

Oh, it subsides ...
  for a little while ...
Til we see someone ...
  who has his smile ...

Or something else ...
  that reminds you of him
Our heart starts to break ...
  Again and again

But you know what...
  I've found a friend ...
Who gives me peace ...
  down deep within ...

He's your friend too
  He's a friend to all...
On His name ...
  you just have to call

He also died young ...
  out of Love for me and you
Now that's a FRIEND!!...
  a friend so true ...

Because of God's Love ...
  we'll see our sons again
Just say, thank you Jesus
  for being our best friend ...

Ennis has the best friend ...
  he has ever had ...
He's happy and at peace ...
  and sends his love to mom and dad

My Heart, Mind and Soul Are In Your Hands Now ... Nicholas

Once again, a voice is silent
  by the hand of the "evil one"
Another youth, to die, so young
  another of God's sons

So many lives, in so few years
  did this young man touch
His light will shine forever
  for he was loved so much

Nicholas loved Jesus Christ
  and wanted his peers to know
Nick was kind and giving to everyone
  through him, God's love glowed

His music was another way
  the Love of God would shine
Prayers for unit on this earth ...
  would fill the music lines

His hatred for violence was evident
  especially for the killings in schools
As for prejudice of any type
  "Moose," thought was so unkool

How so apropos ...
  on the National Day of Prayer
Nicholas was put to rest
  angels rejoicing everywhere

For on that very day
   prayers went out for peace
For Satan to lose our children
   it's he we must defeat

God knows your heart is breaking
   that pain He knows well...
For He gave His Son to die for us
   to save our souls from hell...

God was waiting for Nicholas ...
   with His arms opened wide
"Welcome HOME my loving son ...
   come sit by your Father's side

"Well done my good and faithful servant"
   for my work you did on earth
The evil ones who caused your death ...
   their lives are truly cursed.

Unless they ask for my forgiveness ...
   for they are my children too
Satan has a hold on them
   that's why they killed you

As Christians we all realize
   there will be a glorious day
When we will join our loved ones
   in Heaven, eternally we'll stay

God will help you through this
   I know, for He did me ...
When my son, Ray, also died
   He heard my hurting pleas ...

There's something we all can do ...
   don't let Nick's death be in vain ...
KNOW Jesus as your Lord and Saviour
   or NO Heaven will you gain ....

"Greater Love Has No One Than This, That He Lay Down His Life For His Friends" John 15:13

We are so sorry Moms and Dads
   that we couldn't say goodbye
But we just didn't know
   that day we would die

We know your hearts were broken
   but please don't cry
We know your heart is filled
   with more questions why

We know God didn't cause it
   please know this is true
He wouldn't cause this pain
   for any of you

You know that it is Satan
   who brings evil our way
Through Eric and Dillan
   he came that day

They were consumed with hate
   Isaiah Shoels would say
Let there be no more hate parents
   it is only Satan's way

They listened to Satan's music
  "Doomed" was their favorite Video game
That's how Satan reached them (says Dan)
  for "Power" they would gain

They felt, no one liked them (says Kyle)
  treated like nobodies, they said
They wanted to "SHOW US"
  even if we were all dead!

They didn't care who they killed (says Matthew)
  but they hated us so-called —jocks
And anyone who was known —
  to be in the Christian flock

This was evident (says Cassie)
  when they asked of me
If I loved Jesus —
  I had to say YES — you see

If I had said NO
  and I had not of died
I would've wished that I had
  for my love of Christ denied

I was at peace mom and dad
  when I pledged my love —
For I was already in the arms
  of my Father above

I knew that my "Yes"
  was a death sentence for me
But it wasn't "death" but LIFE
  unlike I never foreseen

I didn't know that my "Yes"
  would late save souls
Bring hundreds of kids
  to Jesus, they didn't know

I thank you mom and dad
  and I love you very much
For continuing in my walk
  for many souls you've touched

Remember my last poem (says Rachael)
  there are no coincidences with God we know
I believe He was preparing us
  for this shocking blow

"The Power is in your hand —
  as to where eternity you spend"
Choose Jesus as your Lord and Saviour
  or Hell will be your end

God was pleased with me (says John)
  For building that house last year
Those poor people in Mexico
  In His heart He holds dear

And thank all the kids for me
  for covering my old chev. with love
It never looked so good
  as I looked from above

Don't let Satan win this battle
  turn this evil into good
Show other kids how to live
  the way that Jesus would

We know you all will be o.k.
　for Jesus told us this
We send our love to all of you
　with a Special Hug and Kiss

We are all doing great (says Steve)
　and I don't need a Pilot license here
I can fly without a plane
　and I have no fear!

We were all scared at first (says Lauren)
　then God sent Angels to us
We knew we were in God's hands
　on Him we could trust

I thought Paris was beautiful (says Daniel)
　but that was nothing to see —
Not compared to this place
　there are streets of gold endlessly!

This place is awesome (says Corey)
　and you should see the "Greens"
And the fish jump out at you but
　No Hunting, Please!

I am sorry I left you family (says Wm. Sanders)
　but I just couldn't stand by
And let them kill my students
　I just had to try

Eric and Dillan pulled the trigger
　but Satan loaded the gun
Each insult from certain kids
　destroyed them — one by one

We will all be waiting
 for that Glorious day
When we greet you at the gate
 eternity with us you'll stay ...

Our Poetic Angel

As I look to the heavens
    for the words for my angel,
I think back on her life
    so amazing this angel

Her Poppa Paul, known as "Shorty"
    her hero til the Lord took him home,
Momma Clara always her strength
    her strong character she always shown

A child so precious
    spunk, her middle name,
Always a character and a dancer
    an actress was her game

A routine, or a short skit
    her and sis Donna would do,
A soft shoe or a song
    not a soul could be blue

Kick the can and red rover
    Potters Park for an ice skate
Games full of laughter
    throw the ball, cross the plate

Dancing the jitter bug
    for money with her big sis,
At Hoppy's Island with friends
    what a sight was this

Yvonne could cut a rug
  as the audience would sing,
"Go Vonnie Go"
  "make this song your own thing"

Cheering for Hamilton Catholic
  Mommas' could lead a cheer
Head cheerleader in the front
  our Vonnie had no fear

Ohio was her home
  until she had to go,
To Florida she did choose
  with her rugrats in tow

Her family always so special
  from her brothers to her sissy's
They gave her such love
  that sustained her like kissy's

Times were never easy
  our life was often a struggle,
But my Mommas did provide
  in her bossom we did snuggle

She gave without thought
  of her own daily needs
Her children and friends came first
  so blessed Mommas deeds

Myself and my sister Lee
  brother Ray and brother Joe
We didn't always have much
  but Mommas love made us grow

A love like no other
  as you all can concur,
She touched all that she knew
  with her love potion she did stir

A waitress with such class
  always a joke and a smile,
"Momma Guildas" to "Nicks Diner"
  she served all, with "Vonnie's style"

Talents, oh so many
  where do I begin,
I guess I'll start by saying
  she was everyone's best friend

She never had an enemy
  for she loved all that walked the earth
From her beautiful dog she treasured
  to her, all life had worth

Smiles, Mommas did always give
  to all the lives she did touch
Never asking for herself
  she always loved so much

Shopping like my Mommas
  now this only she could do,
She could decorate your house for a buck fifty
  and on a good day, your neighbors too!

The world was her canvas
  and she loved her brush
My Mommas, always an artist
  the worlds pain she did hush

A Poem, "Mommas Style"
  what words of love she shared
Never wanting much from life
  but to let all know she cared

So elegant with a flair
  my Mommas style was this,
A beautiful queen with a small joke
  this is who we will miss

A perfect love for the world
  for the man on the street,
To her special neighbor Diane
  my Mommas made life complete

For all those that she met
  be at work, or be at play,
You know this poetic angels love
  with her hats on display

Her friends, she had so many
  as we look around here we can see
My Mommas had such love
  for all the world she gave such glee

Of all my Mommas babies
  I was her first she made with love
The oldest of her four lovely's
  her God smiled from up above

Just a young teenage woman
  she was still a baby herself,
But though her years were young
  her love was only top shelf

Ray her middle son
  the clown of her crew,
He gave her laughter everyday
  and put down a plate or two

Lisa, my beautiful sister
  my Mommas baby girl,
So much love she gave our Mommas
  so much love she gave the world

Joedy her youngest
  her baby who she adored
As Ray, Lisa and I went west
  her love on him she did pour

She never missed his ball games
  Mommas his biggest fan
At times we might have been jealous
  but my brother Joe, was her "little" man

As her Ray-Ray did pass
  her heart did take a toll
To see her son pass first
  made such a big ugly hole

Grandma Clara turns 70
  and oh what a hoot
My precious Mommas as Edith Anne
  grandma laughed in her suit

Grandchildren a "special gift"
  and my mommas had quite a few
The oldest of them was Justin
  the skater of the crew

Then there was Shaun
   Justins little bro,
He could come see mommas for five minutes
   and her stack she could sometimes blow

Jordan came along later
   Joedy's first beautiful boy
Mommas raised him like her own
   Oh, how he gave her so much joy

Alyssa and little Ryan
   Mommas youngest little treasures
From Joe and Gerri, Lisa & Mario
   they gave our Mommas such pleasures

Jesus always Mommas mentor
   her savior and her sweet king,
He gave her the love she shared
   every day undying

As we reflect on this sweet angel
   there is such a loss inside,
But we know her walk with Jesus
   in His hands she now resides

Mommas, My Sweet Mommas
   as we say our good-byes
I just want to say "I Love You"
   to my poetic angel in heavens sky

Gary